Private Passions

Private Passions

*Betraying discipleship
on the journey to Jerusalem*

Douglas J. Davies

CANTERBURY
PRESS
Norwich

© Douglas Davies 2000

First published in 2000 by The Canterbury Press Norwich
(a publishing imprint of Hymns Ancient & Modern Limited
a registered charity)
St Mary's Works, St Mary's Plain
Norwich, Norfolk, NR3 3BH

British Library Cataloguing in Publication Data

A catalogue record of this book is available
from the British Library

ISBN 1-85311-380-8

Typeset by Regent Typesetting, London
Printed in Great Britain by
Cox & Wyman Ltd, Reading, Berkshire

Contents

Foreword by the Archbishop of Wales   vii

Preface   ix

1. Betrayal and Support   1
2. Setting Out and Casting Out   17
3. The Passions of Peter and Pilate   33
4. The Passion of Judas   49
5. The Supper   60
6. The Garden Betrayal   77
7. Paul's Passion   88
8. The Death of Christ   97
9. Death's Passion   110
10. In Praise of Passion   121

Points for Discussion and Reflection   127

Bibliography   131

Index   132

Foreword

As Douglas Davies reminds us, every time Christians of some traditions celebrate Holy Communion, they recall the fact that Jesus Christ was betrayed by those who had been closest to him. And this should suggest to us that we, who believe we are close to the Lord, are no less capable of betrayal. Douglas Davies helps us to think about our capacity for betrayal by reflecting on the betrayals that are recounted in the gospels, putting to us the disturbing question of whether Judas might be seen as the typical Christian – turning against Christ when Christ disappoints his expectations, and finding in the process that his own unfaithfulness destroys him.

As this indicates, Professor Davies also wants us to think about how the passion of Christ is linked to our own 'passions' – our emotions, our fantasies, our suffering, our sense of being trapped. He deliberately keeps us close to the tragedy, so that the good news of Easter never becomes a cheap happy ending, but truly is new life out of real death.

Written with great clarity and care, this book opens up all kinds of new perspectives on the Passion story, and should be an excellent aid to Bible study, in groups or alone. Professor Davies goes to the heart of this central mystery of our faith in showing how the community of betrayers becomes the community that trusts and is trusted, bound together by the shared experience of failure and the shared experience of forgiveness through the Passion of Jesus.

Rowan Williams
October 2000

Preface

One of the books I value most carries inside its front cover a presentation message reminding me that it was a Gwynno James Memorial Prize for 1973 from the Diocese of Llandaff. At that time I was an ordinand of the Church in Wales studying theology at Durham after some years spent as a student of anthropology. I have always been grateful for that support as well as for the encouragement provided in my home village of Bedlinog and its parish of St Cadoc. I am also reminded of the gentle guidance of Archbishop Glyn Simon.

Circumstances were such that I became a university teacher and, with my first post at the University of Nottingham, I was ordained in the Diocese of Southwell where I served in a number of urban and rural parishes for over 20 years as a non-stipendiary priest. In 1997 I returned to Durham where I am now Professor in the Study of Religion in the Department of Theology. This book has been largely written at my old College of St John's where I have been pleased to hold a Research Fellowship this year. I thank its Principal, Bishop Stephen Sykes, and other members of College for their hospitality and, in particular, Dr James Saunders, an ordinand at Cranmer Hall, who has carefully read the typescript. I would also like to thank Mr McKinnell of Durham's Department of English and the Chapter of Durham

Cathedral for permission to reproduce their Judas Cup Ceremony.

Finally, let me say how pleased I am to have been invited to write The Archbishop's Lent Book for 2001. It has prompted me to think about topics that might otherwise never have attracted my attention and also enables me to thank family and friends in Wales for so much over so many years.

Douglas J. Davies
University of Durham
Trinity 2000

I

Betrayal and Support

Jesus was not only betrayed by Judas, but by Peter and Pilate, by his other disciples and by Paul, just as he has been betrayed by many of his followers down to this day. This book is about some of those betrayals and their impact upon betrayer and betrayed, for betrayal is a two-edged sword. Jesus was not, however, betrayed by his mother Mary, nor, in John's Gospel at least, by his 'beloved disciple'. These exceptions form part of the mixed yet compelling picture of the life and Passion of Jesus as experienced, remembered and recorded by groups of early Christians in the New Testament. From the Gospels and epistles there emerges a picture of a community that had known the impact of betrayal, had lived through it and emerged as a community of grace. This particular transformation from betrayal to grace has often been ignored in studies of the Bible and offers fresh opportunities for understanding the power of earliest Christianity. In this book I will only undertake a small part of this exploration by focusing almost entirely on the betrayals underlying the suffering and death of Jesus.

Betrayal Behaviours

The events described in the following chapters do not always appear as straightforward examples of betrayal but, for the purpose of this book, I will bring them together as a cluster of behaviours, each bearing a certain family resemblance to the others. They comprise an unmistakable pattern of betrayal, denial, rejection, certain forms of judgement, and abandonment. We can also think of these actions as forming a scale: from being of relatively slight importance to being totally serious in their impact upon an individual. As far as Jesus is concerned, I will suggest that at one end of the scale there is the rich young ruler deciding not to join Jesus in his journey to Jerusalem, while at the other end Jesus sees himself as forsaken by God. Along the scale are Peter, James and John, Pilate and Paul. Some people will find it odd, perhaps even wrong, to include God in this list and yet the Gospel accounts stand witness to the death of Jesus and to his words from the cross which we must take with some seriousness. Some will also find it strange to talk about Paul in connection with the sufferings of Christ. All this will become clear in the following pages as we are challenged to think again about that journey taken by the man from Nazareth who set his face to travel to Jerusalem with a band of disciples who still only half understood the mission of their Rabbi.

This book not only is about the Bible and events of the past, but also concerns their significance for today's life and faith. It links the experiences of the early disciples with our own half-understandings and our journey to personal places of trial. It is about us as individuals who may have been betrayed and who may have betrayed others. Our task is to see the Gospel stories come alive through insights into our own situations as we are drawn into what befell Jesus in his day. His life and ours become involved with each other. We will see the Gospels as being written by people of faith for people of faith. Above all we will encounter a realistic world of mistakes and failures where people hurt others and are hurt themselves.

Passions and Passion

The central focus of this book is that of 'passion', a word used here not in its ordinary meaning of strong emotions and commitments but in its more specifically Christian sense of the suffering of Jesus immediately before his crucifixion and death. That suffering came to be seen by believers as crucial to their salvation and, because of this, the Passion of Christ became part of the yearly cycle of worship and meditation. The Sunday before Palm Sunday was often called Passion Sunday, and highlighted the events involved in his suffering, events that will be described throughout this book. More recently, Passion Sunday and Palm Sunday have come to be combined in some churches as the Sunday beginning the week that leads into Easter and includes Maundy Thursday and Good Friday before passing over Easter Eve into Easter Day.

However, this book cannot only be about the Passion of Jesus. It must also speak of those individuals with whom he lived, especially those caught up in his life and in the mission he saw lying before him. This not only applies to his actual disciples, and those involved in his trial and death, but also to the millions of individuals who have found their own lives touched by the life of Jesus of Nazareth. So I will also speak, for example, of the passions of Peter, Pilate, Judas and, not least, of our own passion. I assume that many who read this book will, to some degree or other, use it as one way of thinking about their own life, its misfortunes, sorrows and sufferings. If there is a strong emphasis upon the more negative aspects of life in this book it is not because Christianity is without joy, hope and love, but because there is a place for taking seriously these other emotional depths. This is particularly true at that time of the year when the sufferings of Christ are presented to us in the devotional life of the Church.

Some who read this book will be devout Christians and some will wonder if they are Christian at all. Some will have suffered a great deal while others will not, yet at least, have experienced the depths of physical, mental or emotional pain. Life is a mysterious process and we often do not know what is to meet us tomorrow – whether great joy or sorrow or the more usual ups and downs of daily experience. What is certainly the case is that we are all in this world together, a fact reflected in that odd mix of community called the Church. It is just this sense of togetherness that helps us see how one life affects another and invites us to consider our own passions in relation to those of Jesus, of his disciples and of those he met. Above all else, the Christian Church, through its many denominations and branches, forms a great group; a group of many groups, of men and women, boys and girls seeking to live in relation to Jesus, to his teaching and his life.

Church and Churches

Ideally, the Church should achieve several crucial goals. At the personal and emotional levels it needs to be a community of encouragement, support and strength for its individual members. Because it is concerned with truth, it is also committed to learning and to that kind of self-discovery that produces an increasing maturity of understanding as the years go by. In that way it fosters the ethical life of individuals and societies. A church is also a place of worship where believers are, as it were, taken out of themselves as they relate to God and to each other. In the process they are enabled to gain a sounder perspective on their own lives. Because the Christian Church deals with all these most vital aspects of life it can easily slip into obsessions and preoccupations. It can take itself too seriously and view its own ways as the only true ways. Because it holds high ideals it can be a sad home for those who make mistakes. But, above all, it is a place committed to seeing God's ways prevail in the full knowledge that this is never fully achieved because the Churches are human institutions despite their divine desires. This is never so clear as when we look at the life of Jesus and of his earliest followers. There, too, we find shattered hopes, misunderstood intentions and the frailty of human commitments as the New Testament writers fully describe failure. Nothing is hidden. Here lies one key for faith today, a key that comes with the opportunity to take a little time – perhaps especially in the weeks of Lent that move from Ash Wednesday through to Good Friday and to Easter Eve – to ponder the life of Jesus and our own lives.

Journey to Jerusalem

I shall relate the story of Jesus as he sets his face to go up to Jerusalem to meet what lies before him. Using the different Gospel accounts we explore the spectrum of experience that befell not only Jesus but also numerous individuals whose lives were caught up with him in those fateful days. In so doing we will, inevitably, find ourselves considering our own situations and experiences, for we all encounter suffering and pain of some sort. Whether mental or physical, these experiences involve other people and furnish their own kinds of passion. I will look at the passions of the central actors in the Gospel accounts of the final phase of Christ's earthly ministry, and will talk about the various ways in which they neglected or rejected the journey Jesus took to Jerusalem. His disciples were to be his companions along the way, but events transpired to betray this journey and Jesus as the one undertaking it. In the process people also betrayed themselves.

By keeping this very phrase, 'betraying the journey', before our mind's eye as we consider the biblical events, stories and interpretations explored in the following chapters, we may, perhaps, be helped to reflect upon our own faith. The idea of a journey has, of course, long been a popular way of thinking about life itself. But that is not the reason why it has been chosen as our guideline: it is all too obvious that life can be seen as a journey. Rather, it is the New Testament accounts of Jesus in his last weeks that prompt, even demand, that we see his life's purpose coming to its climax in the journey to Jerusalem. The same texts that throw new light on the crucial events of this progression to the Holy City also illustrate the betrayal of that journey. Through the eyes of the Gospel writers they not only furnish us with the image of 'betraying the journey' but also provide our invitation to join Jesus, his disciples and others to see our own lives in theirs. We see their commitments as ours: we see them being betrayed and betraying and suddenly we see how easily we too are betrayers and betrayed. As one way of summarizing and drawing together these various aspects of betrayal I will use the phrase 'cluster of betrayal' to describe them all together.

Interpreting Gospel and Gospels

To accept this invitation is to take on a detailed study of the ways in which the four Gospels and other parts of the Bible deal with the key events in Jesus' life. This will demonstrate that things are not always quite as simple as the mental pictures we make of them. To do justice to these complex matters, there is a real need to stand back a little from what may be our own familiar images of such events as Jesus entering Jerusalem on a donkey, or the Last Supper, or the

Garden of Gethsemane, or even the Crucifixion. It is so easy to read our own meanings and feelings into the Bible due to our familiarity with the passages concerned or because our knowledge of the Bible may not be very extensive. Often we are left to work with half-remembered stories from Sunday School, or from a film or a sermon that once sketched the subject. In the following chapters we will have a greater opportunity to stand back from our familiar understanding of the Bible as we compare the different Gospel stories and other accounts of the events surrounding Jesus' suffering and death. This is not an easy task, but it is a challenge that will repay the effort.

One basic difficulty stems from an image of the Bible that can, ironically, often be gained from church or from personal Bible reading. It comes from thinking of the Bible as a simple and direct text that gives a plain account of what really happened to the people described in its pages. Detailed study can bring us to see that these accounts are, actually, deeply influenced by the biblical writers who emphasize one feature or omit others in order to make their own point. In other words, the biblical texts were written by individuals with a real faith of their own, with a particular grasp of the significance of Jesus and of what they believed God was doing through him. For some, this sort of analysis can come as a disappointment and lead to a degree of disillusion either with the Bible itself or with the scholars who present it in this kind of way. One reaction ignores this view altogether and simply affirms the simple truth of the Bible. This view can easily lead to a kind of fundamentalism, of taking the Bible as 'literally true', and of seeing the very idea of 'interpreting the Bible' as a faithless and false way of doing things.

Although I can understand this reaction, I think it is unfortunate for one particular reason: it hides the fact that the Bible was written by fellow believers who, in their day and age, were coming to grips with what faith meant to them, and wanted to share it with others. They were not simply some kind of neutral channel through which God placed words on paper. Throughout this book we see how the Gospel writers each give a different version and interpretation of events. They want us to grasp particular truths, truths that had meant a great deal to them and to the Christian groups to which they belonged and within which their own faith had been formed. To know that the Bible was written by people of faith for the faith of other people is to see the power of interpretation and the great need to give ourselves to it in our own day.

Synoptic Gospels and John

With that in mind it is important to remember the difference that exists between the Gospels of Matthew, Mark and Luke on the one hand and John's Gospel on the other. Matthew, Mark and Luke are often called the Synoptic Gospels or the Synoptics because they present a kind of synopsis or shared outlook on the overall story of events. Many scholars think that Mark's Gospel was the earliest of all the Gospels and that Matthew and Luke used it as a kind of skeleton of the story of Jesus' life, working into it and developing from it their own special insight into the significance of it all. Matthew, for his part, draws out strong links with the Jewish background and origins of Jesus and his mission. Luke has his own eye set on the power of the Holy Spirit and on all that was to happen in the other book that many believe he wrote: the Acts of the Apostles. Nevertheless, the great majority of events and episodes present in Mark are also present in Matthew and Luke. However, this is not the case in John's Gospel. John has an entire set of ideas and images of Jesus that are not found in the synoptic vision of Matthew, Mark and Luke. These similarities and differences will become apparent throughout the following chapters and will provide the opportunity for seeing how the Christian faith emerged in the various communities in which the Gospel writers experienced the faith for themselves.

Faith Communities

This is an important issue because we are not approaching the Gospels as some simple form of history where we can read the facts in any simple way. Just as the Gospel writers each used their own form of interpretation of events in the life of Jesus we, too, come to their writings to interpret them for ourselves. Here the question of faith is important because the accounts of Jesus' life, and most especially of his Passion, have their home among Christian peoples, among all sorts of Christian people. They in turn influence and shape the faith of those individuals and the groups to which they belong. It is precisely within individual lives and the networks of friends that make up the living hearts of churches that these narratives live. This is one reason why it seems much better to talk about Gospel narratives rather than about Gospel stories, because stories suggest fiction or entertainment and the Gospels strike believers in quite a different way from that. It is all a question of perspective and purpose. The perspective in this book is on the life of Jesus as a Passion, as a committed life with emotional depths reaching into the heartland of human existence before God. Our purpose is so to interpret his life as to gain an increasing awareness of our own. I am assuming that one reason we are attracted to the Passion of Christ is because in some way, degree or kind we have a passion of our own. Although we are 2000 years away from the writers of the Gospels their insight is not 2000 years away from us. There is a very odd sense in which, despite all historical analysis and scientific discoveries, the human heart still speaks to heart.

Throughout the following chapters our attention will, then, be drawn ever closer to the devastating theme of betrayal, an experience lying at the very heart of Jesus and his life with the disciples and yet one that has, generally, occupied a limited place in Christian thinking. This is even true when we reflect upon what is traditionally called the Passion of Christ. For whatever reason, that state of affairs needs to be corrected if we are to meet two challenges: first, to picture Jesus as he sets out to fulfil the tasks he sees lying before him; and second, on a more personal level, to relate those events of the Gospel narratives to our own life and existence.

Distance and Perspective

These difficult tasks require persistence and a degree of honesty in trying to see what the biblical texts actually say rather than what we think they say. Familiarity can serve many purposes apart from contempt. It can be a great service when well-known hymns and the words of liturgy help us to worship more freely because we are neither lost for words nor stumbling over new ones. But familiarity can also hide treasures from us for, sometimes, when we glimpse things from a slightly different direction the familiar story becomes a new revelation. This is the challenge with the Passion of Christ, and the phrase 'betraying the journey' will be the key to open a slightly unfamiliar way of approaching the experience of Jesus so often pondered by Christians as they prepare for Easter.

Of course we must admit at the very outset that we are far from knowing how Jesus felt about his life and the events that befell him for he never wrote any letters or Gospels. The best we can do is to take up what his early followers said of him and to explore their own insights and faith through the different words and rearrangement of events provided in the Gospels to express particular messages. The question of interpretation in the widest sense remains very important; we know that caution needs to frame our opinions, not least the great emphasis placed in this book upon betrayal. There is a real sense in which if Jesus of Nazareth appeared today in our local congregation, as though by miracle, we would not be able to understand what he said: we would need an interpreter. What I mean is the obvious fact that Jesus, as a man, spoke no English, Welsh, Italian or any other widely used modern language. Very few people today understand the Aramaic language spoken by Jesus, just as few Christians understand the Greek of the New Testament or the Hebrew of the Old Testament. The distance between twenty-first-century Christians and first-century followers of Jesus is very great indeed, even though this gap is often hidden through the prayers, hymns and personal thoughts of Jesus that operate through our own language. So we tend to think of Jesus of Nazareth as one who would, of course, be intelligible to us. Through the community of believers the gap of history has been closed.

It is with this in mind that we approach these accounts of Jesus, his disciples and the others caught up with his mission. But we do not approach them neutrally, as casual observers of a street theatre, but as people with our own experiences, needs, hopes and ambitions, and as those informed by today's Christian communities. That is why the following chapters explore alongside the Passion of

Jesus the passions of Peter, Pilate, Judas and Paul, never forgetting that we, too, have passions of our own. Whether lying behind us in times of great hardship or pain, or lying in front of us, we are not ignorant of what it means to suffer within ourselves and through our relationships with those close to us. It is on the assumption that your life and mine echo, in however small or great a way, the passions of the Gospels that we set out to read them into our lives and to read our lives into them.

As we do this we will find ourselves doing theology. We will be thinking about God and about ourselves and the nature of the life we lead. We will be alert to the aims and motives of the Gospel writers and aware of the communities in which they lived and from which they wrote their documents. We will never forget the divide of time and cultures that separate us but neither will we forget the common humanity and the tradition of faith that we share. Above all we know that, whether in the past or present, people engage with the life of Christ as part of their faith and do so through belonging to these strange groups called churches which, century after century, tell the stories and proclaim the faith. To be part of this is a great adventure and privilege but it is also challenging and almost frightening. One thing is certain: the following chapters will not always be comforting. Perhaps we already know too well what it means to 'betray the journey', even before we spell out the implications of this disturbing phrase. Perhaps that is why betrayal holds a low profile in Christian reflection upon the Gospel passions, and equally why it is the very reason we need to do it when we reflect upon the breadth of faith and life, not least during the season of Lent.

Lent

As a brief background it is worth knowing that Lent has risen and fallen in popularity over the centuries and in different churches. A period of discipline, especially involving fasting, seems to have been established by about 300 years after the death of Jesus and may well have been part of the preparation for the great rite of baptism that took place at Easter. Just as the time of resurrection was the appropriate time for baptism and entering into new life as a Christian, so the period running up to it was one of preparation and control of the physical body. The period came to be associated with a 40-day timescale, one that reflected biblical ideas of figures such as Moses and Jesus who underwent fasts. When the Reformation led to the establishment of the Church of England in the sixteenth century there was some debate over whether fasting and Lent should be maintained or abolished. The general view was that Lent should be retained with fasting seen as a positive benefit, though it then tended to fall into disuse and was only revived in the nineteenth century. Today it seems as though there might be something of a revival of interest in Lent as a period of religious reflection.

Mary

At the very outset of our study of this journey to Jerusalem it is important to make it clear that, while our stress on betrayal does reflect a strong current in early Christian thought, it is not the only possible view. There is another tradition, largely present in John's Gospel, in which Mary, the mother of Jesus, and the 'beloved disciple' are shown not to have betrayed or abandoned Jesus in his hour of death. Even so, these two views are closely related as a brief sketch of Mary will make clear.

Mary, like the others we will consider later, possessed a private passion, but unlike the others she stands out from them by not being part of the cluster of betrayal. Rather, she shares in it to her personal cost. Luke's is the Gospel that first introduces us to Mary and to her bond with Jesus. As part of the narrative of his birth, Luke tells how his parents take the infant Jesus to Jerusalem for his circumcision. An old and godly man, Simeon, sees the child in the temple, takes him in his arms and proclaims what, traditionally, we have come to call the Nunc Dimittis. This Latin phrase has come to be the name for the hymn often used in church services which begins, 'O Lord now lettest thou thy servant depart in peace, according to thy word, for my eyes have seen thy salvation'. At the close of that text Simeon addresses Mary, saying that Jesus is set 'for the fall and rise of many in Israel' and that he will be a 'sign that is spoken against'. Words are then added to the text in a rather odd way, almost like an intruded thought, as Simeon says to Mary, 'and a sword will pierce through your heart also' (Luke 2:35).

Here, at the outset of Luke's Gospel, we find the theme of this book: the rejection of Jesus and the pain that will involve many. His Passion will create passion for others. Mary's suffering is expressed in the extremely powerful language of a sword piercing her own heart also. The Greek is very strong and emphasizes that it is her own life that will be torn apart by forthcoming events, just as the Jewish people themselves will be divided by their response to Jesus. In these verses we gain a picture of people 'falling' and 'rising'. This pattern appears throughout the Gospels as Jesus is followed by those who abandon, deny, betray and reject him but who also later come to follow him anew. In that sense they both 'fall' and 'rise' as disciples of Christ. The overall theme is of the Messiah being rejected by God's people and this theme is then mirrored at the more individual level in the denial of Jesus by his own followers. With Mary the general idea of God's disobedient people rejecting God's anointed one becomes personal and intimate. 'The anguish that Mary would share at the general rejection of her Son' would be great as she witnessed it coming to a culmination in his passion (Marshall 1978: 123). In terms of Christian belief, Mary demonstrates the crucial fact that God's dealing with humanity involves individual human beings and the dynamics of each of their lives. She is to suffer because Jesus suffers.

Throughout the Gospel narratives there is no indication that Mary had ever abandoned, betrayed or denied her son. If anything, there is a suggestion that Jesus seemed to move away from her and the other members of his family as he became increasingly focused on his mission. Indeed, that is even foreshadowed in the event of the boy Jesus staying on at the temple while his parents go on home and, in a sense, lose him (Luke 2:21–40). There is also the occasion when they come to meet him and cannot get to him because of the crowd. When Jesus is told they want to see him it triggers his question as to who his mother and brothers are. He answers that it is those who do the will of his Father in heaven. Still, the fact that she is described as one of those who wait and watch with Jesus at his Crucifixion attests to her ongoing support, as also that of some of the other women associated with Jesus in his life and work. John's Gospel has Mary even more closely involved with the death of Jesus and also with the 'beloved disciple', to whom I return in a later chapter. Nowhere is Mary part of any idea of abandonment but, in this, she is an exception in the Synoptic Gospels. So it is that, as one commentator expressed it, 'the chord struck here' over rejection 'would be orchestrated in many ways' as the

Gospel stories spelled out the life and destiny of Jesus (Fitzmyer 1981: 423). And so it will be throughout the remaining chapters of this book where the Passion of Christ confronts, challenges and supports the private passions of our own lives.

Setting Out and Casting Out

To see the journey of a lifetime lying at the heart of the Gospels as a journey of betrayal is to begin to understand the Passion of Christ and of those caught up in the events of his life, teaching and death. Let Mark's Gospel be our prime guide for this difficult journey, but with the other Gospels helping to illuminate particular stops along the way and, occasionally, having to bear the sole responsibility for particular episodes. It would be very easy for us to call this a journey of salvation and to highlight the many features with which we are already familiar: landmarks often pointed out when this ground is covered in sermons or study groups. But many of the key events occur in the dark world of a night-journey, where the power of the shadow-side of life is felt. This chapter reveals several aspects of the cluster of betrayal, involving Peter's rebuke of Christ, the sad response of the rich young ruler, the ambitions of James and John, the greedy life of temple merchants and, by sharp contrast, the generous gift of an insightful woman.

We begin early in the Gospels, shortly after Jesus has chosen his disciples, healed the sick and taught through many parables. Peter responds to that question posed by Jesus – 'Who do men say that I am?' – with his memorable words: 'Thou art the Christ' (Mark 8:29). This becomes a turning point of the Gospel with a transition from miracles to the journey. Jesus now teaches his disciples that suffering and rejection lie ahead. It is as though everything falls into chaos for a moment. Jesus asks his disciples who people say that he is. Peter announces him as the Christ. Once that is out in the open he spells out the consequences as he sees them but Peter will have none of it and rebukes Jesus who, 'seeing his disciples', in turn rebukes Peter and calls him Satan. This is a remarkable turn of events! In fact our familiarity with the Bible probably hides the strength of that exchange between these two men. It is almost impossible not to feel sorry for Peter. One moment his words are profound in their recognition of Jesus and the next moment they are in opposition to him. He is right about the identity of Jesus but wrong about his mission of Jesus as the Christ, the anointed one who is to establish God's kingdom. So much is packed into that brief phrase used by Jesus when he is rebuked by Peter. Jesus turns and, 'seeing his disciples', he turns the tables and rebukes Peter in the unforgettable words: 'Get behind me Satan! For you are not on the side of God but of men' (Mark 8:33). His disciples were not to be deceived. They should not be misled by Peter's labelling of Jesus as the Christ nor lulled into a false sense of security over the implication of that identity. Their prospects as his disciples needed spelling out. And this, Mark tells us, was done incisively as Jesus calls his disciples together to tell them that if they follow him they must take up their cross; they must lose their life if they are to find it.

There then follows a series of strange events that demonstrate a world of mixed messages, hopes and fears. This period surrounding the serious start of a serious journey is far from simple. There is a gathering of emotion, a build-up of spiritual tension that will only be released once the goal is attained. The immediate outcome is the Transfiguration of Jesus. Now that his disciples have some inkling of the realistic truth of what lies ahead, three of them accompany Jesus to a mountain. There they see him talking with Elijah and Moses, great symbols of God's dealings with their Jewish ancestors, and it is as though he glows while a divine voice announces that he is 'my beloved son' (Mark 9:7). Then, all of a sudden, the vision vanishes and Jesus is alone with them. More healing miracles follow, along with further teaching that 'The Son of man will be delivered into the hands of sinful men' who will kill him, though he will be raised again. Mark explicitly adds that they did not understand what Jesus was saying but, this time, they were 'afraid to ask him' (Mark 9:30–33). Amid this embarrassed confusion Jesus finds them discussing among themselves who was the greatest. He takes a child to clarify the fact that the greatest is the least, the servant of the rest. Once more, expectations and values are shown to be confused. It is then, after another episode with children, that he clearly tells them that the Kingdom of God must be received as one receives a child. Not that they should be childish or simple or any such thing but that they should not rebuke it, or send it away, but rather welcome it (Mark 10:15).

Youthful, Sad Clarity

That message comes immediately into sharp focus when a rich young man runs up to Jesus, kneels and asks how he may inherit eternal life. Here was an honest person. Jesus saw his sincerity and told him to give his wealth away and to follow him. This the youth was unable to do, and he went away sorrowing, 'for he had great possessions' (Mark 10:22). There is something quite crucial about this particular encounter that paves the way for the journey of betrayal, for Mark's text indicates that it was just as Jesus 'was setting out on his journey' that the young man ran up to him. The picture is of a departure. If we imagined this event to have taken place in the modern age of railways it would have been just as the train, with Jesus on it, was drawing away from the platform that a bustle would have occurred on the platform with the youth running to speak to Jesus. The brief conversation would be held, and the truth would be told, with the inquirer being invited to leave all behind and to jump on the train. But that scene would have ended with the train drawing away from the station leaving a growing gap between the two of them. In the Gospel story Jesus turns to his disciples, to those on the journey with him, and tells them yet again that much is gained when encumbrances, whether of wealth or even of family, are left behind for his sake (Mark 10:23–33).

This case of the rich young man should, perhaps, be taken to represent the very commencement of Christ's Passion, at least as we are pursuing it in this book, as the passion of betrayal. For that youth, as full of sincerity as he was imbued with wealth, came to one whom he was convinced knew the answer to his deepest question about life and destiny. He heard the answer, knew its significance, and then departed. Jesus looked at him, as Mark's Gospel clearly asserts, and loved him. Here was someone Jesus would have wished to have join his last journey as a companion in the truth; someone who, even in his brief contact with Jesus, had seen the implications of the answer the Master gave him. Unlike the surrounding debates of the disciples over which of them was the greatest or what they might receive in the light of all they had given up to follow Jesus, this individual knew the score.

This turning away presents us with the first rejection of Jesus at the very outset of his journey to Jerusalem. While it would, certainly, be excessive to describe this event as a betrayal it does bear some of the elements of the betrayals that are to follow. For, clearly, there is something of a bond between the two individuals, created even through such a brief encounter. Jesus is concerned for this person: he knows that they are both set upon a similar venture of engaging with the spirit of divine commandments and not simply with the letter of the law. These two see eye to eye and there is a real degree of understanding between them. And yet, despite his insight, the one described by Luke as a ruler decides against the venture (Luke 18:18). So it is that, at its very outset, the journey to Jerusalem begins with a rejection, an incipient denial, a betrayal in embryo: it leaves no need for any distinction or parallel to be drawn between this individual and Christians at large as far as wealth and the like are concerned (Schweizer 1971: 213).

Amazed Fear

Mark's text then takes us straight back not only to the physical journey but also to the complex emotions surrounding its commencement: 'And they were on the road, going up to Jerusalem, and Jesus was walking ahead of them; and they were amazed, and those who followed were afraid' (Mark 10:32). Mark does his best to indicate the mixed feelings surrounding what is, in effect, the beginning of Christ's Passion. Complexity and uncertainty combine with personal hopes and aspirations, all within the disciples' sense of the motivating purpose pressing Jesus to go to Jerusalem. Mark's language shows that, as a Gospel writer, he sees in Jesus one who knows that the future is one of great hardship and, while he does refer to the Resurrection, his major emphasis falls upon Jesus being handed over to the authorities, condemned, mocked and killed.

But in those brief references to the amazement and fear of the disciples as they followed Jesus on the road going up to Jerusalem, Mark packs deep significance. There is an astonishment at the heart of this emotion, an astonishment that shades into fear. It is deeply reminiscent of those religious experiences described in Rudolph Otto's book *The Idea of the Holy,* which he called the 'numinous' or some mysterious thing that fascinates, attracts and frightens us all at the same time (1924: 97–112). Strangely, while Otto talks about such numinous elements in the New Testament he misses this particular episode in the Gospels. Yet with Mark we glimpse, for a moment, that combination of hope and fear focused on the leader, on Jesus of Nazareth, who now turns himself with real determination to press his message home at the heart of Jewish religious life in Jerusalem. His disciples follow, aware that they are in the company of a great man, the greatest they have ever met, perhaps even the great leader that their fathers and ancestors had long awaited. Perhaps they were also increasingly aware that they had not fully understood his plans or their part in them. It is not surprising, then, that they were amazed and afraid. To be part of something that is far bigger than oneself, with implications and consequences that reach beyond one's own understanding and control, is sufficient cause for fear. But the element of amazement introduces an entirely different dimension. In Mark's Gospel this amazement starts early on when Jesus visits the synagogue at Capernaum where a miracle of healing occurs but where, more to the point, Jesus is reckoned to be one who teaches 'with authority' (Mark 1:27). Cases of amazement, surprise and astonishment then continue, quite extensively, throughout the Gospel and cannot be easily explained as moments when people are either coming to faith or being offended by the message of Jesus (Cranfield 1966: 73). More than that, these moods hint at the way in which Jesus frightened (if that is the right word) and yet attracted the disciples at one and the same time. This is an idea that some find puzzling, especially if they picture Jesus as a kind and loving individual faithfully followed by his devoted disciples. The picture of the Passion of Jesus, as now it begins to unfold, hints at a man with a calling and a destiny that are being pursued and explored by himself with a call to his disciples to be a part of it all. In this there is some uncertainty, an openness towards what lies ahead. And this is how we approach it here, not by trying to stand back and take the wide picture, as people who already know the outcome, but as twenty-first-century people trying to step into line with those disciples following behind him on that road to Jerusalem.

Impossible Passion

Certainly, the disciples were caught up in something that overstretched their imagination, yet they moved ahead with it, for there was something in Jesus, his sense of purpose and of pressing ahead that demanded that they follow. There were moments when the disciples felt in control, as when Peter initially sought to deflect Jesus from the path of pain, and when James and John sought places of honour in the forthcoming Kingdom. Their story links the middle of Mark's Gospel with the final Passion, paving the way with that poignant question from Jesus, 'Are you able to drink the cup I drink?' (Mark 10:38). James and John seem to presume upon Jesus. Perhaps Mark expects us to sympathize with their attitude because he has already described to us their privileged experience of being with Jesus when he was transfigured. Perhaps, too, Mark wants us to think rather along the same lines as James and John, whose experience of Jesus 'in his glory' was of a transformed hero in the company of the nation's greatest of

God's servants. The seats they want are seats of glory. Just as they had thought it good to be with him on the mountain of transfiguration so it would be good, in their anticipation, to be with him in his glory. But that, said Jesus, was not within his power to give.

This was no easy phrase that allows Jesus to escape the request, far from it: rather, it strikes the dominant note of the passion journey that things will happen to people over which they will have no control. In the most literal sense each will be subject to forces that are brought to bear upon them. Passion means that the individual is not in control of events; one is passive in the face of the actions of others or of circumstances. This additional story of James and John wanting pride of place with Christ 'in his glory' merely displays even more clearly the ignorance of the disciples and leads Jesus to teach, yet again, the truth that 'the Son of Man also came not to be served but to serve and to give his life as a ransom for many', as they will soon find out (Mark 10:45). As though to make the point that insight is demanded of the disciples, Mark provides the brief story of blind Bartimaeus, healed by Jesus, who does come to 'see' in more ways than one but who, unlike the rich man, does end up 'following on the way' (Mark 10:52).

Jerusalem: Passion's Destination

So the contrast is drawn. The rich man leaves, the poor man follows, as they draw near to Jerusalem where Jesus will expand on his teaching. But first he makes that entry on the donkey, welcomed by the crowds, and he makes an entry into the temple to drive out its traders. We are told that the authorities wanted him killed, 'for they feared him, because all the multitude was astonished at his teaching' (Mark 11:18). Here fear among the chief priests is contrasted with the astonishment of the crowds. Mark 12 sets the scene for the final encounter between Jesus and the authorities, with the latter awaiting an appropriate opportunity to arrest him out of sight of his supportive public. But before that aggressive encounter there remain other events, rich in intimacy and distance, in depth and shallowness of relationships, and in the disclosure and hiding of the real nature of his journey to Jerusalem. These begin with the anointing with perfume.

Glorious Wastefulness

This event involves what we might call the passion of this beautiful thing. It is an example that contradicts the cluster of betrayal and yet provides an opportunity for us to glimpse an aspect of its negative power. There sits Jesus, receiving the hospitality at the house of one Simon the Leper, when a woman anoints him with a costly fragrance, an act that raises the objection of its expense. Just as the disciples had tried to stop children coming to Jesus so now some chide the woman for expending this upon him. In both cases Jesus prevents their carping and, just as he welcomes the children, so he welcomes her concern for him with the incisive and profoundly telling affirmation that the real meaning of the act is that she has anointed him for burial (Mark 14:8). 'She has done what she could.' We can only speculate on her motive for this. Perhaps Mark might want us to think a little of this anointing as the marking of the Messiah, the Christ, the Anointed One, but equally her insight into his work, her grasp of the general public's approval and yet also of the gossip concerning the religious authorities may all have led her to see the trouble that would lie ahead. Here and now, for the moment, she did what she could. Situations change fast for, unlike the poor,

Jesus will not always be with them. And so it is that Jesus says, 'She has done a beautiful thing to me'. If, as we may assume, Jesus had very strong thoughts about what lay ahead, thoughts that were far from joyous and, equally, if he had some idea of the way his followers would actually treat him when the pressure came on (and he knew them well enough to anticipate that) then this moment stood out as an oasis in a personal desert. Here was someone lavishing attention on him, spending something like a year's worth of a labourer's wage in a moment (Matthew 20:2). How this will contrast with his close disciples' inattention in a day's time when he asks them to support him in his moment of deep anxiety, and how it contrasted with Judas who is introduced in the very next verse of Mark as he leaves to betray Jesus! Here Mark's Gospel is particularly profound, for it links two quite different and entirely opposite things in the subtlest of ways. First it says that what the woman does will always be remembered, 'wherever the gospel is preached in the whole world': just as it has been and is now, once again, in this very chapter. Second, it announces 'Judas Iscariot'. In other words there are two people who will never be forgotten: this woman and her beautiful act and Judas and his act of betrayal. But Mark's Gospel is even more direct in establishing sharp contrasts over the value placed on Jesus, for just as the woman 'wastes' much money on Jesus so Judas is promised money to betray him. Moreover, it is precisely at that very moment when the woman anoints Jesus 'for his burial' that Judas exits to betray him.

In John's Gospel this account of the anointing takes place earlier, before Jesus enters Jerusalem to be greeted with palms and acclamations. It is also given an even greater connection with death in that it is Mary, the sister of Lazarus, whom Jesus raised from the dead, and indeed it

is in their house that the anointing occurs (John 12:1–11).
The link with Lazarus makes death a much closer topic and
even accentuates the fact that Jesus, the one who gave life
to Lazarus, will die. In that account it is also Judas who
objects to the waste of money over the ointment. As far as
the movement of Mark's Gospel is concerned Jesus is now
set upon his journey and the hospitality in Bethany is
temporary and behind him. Here we witness a parting
gesture, a sign of movement as he progresses on his way to
Jerusalem where the passion of friendship awaits him and
those close to him.

Entering Jerusalem

So Jerusalem, the Holy City, comes to be the main focus of
Christ's Passion. The Gospel writers speak of it as more
than a city, more than a place where many people live. For
them it is a double symbol expressing God's promise and
human failure. Nowhere is this more clearly expressed
than in the extremely odd and mixed lament Jesus makes
over Jerusalem (Matthew 23:37–39; Luke 13:34–35). On
the one hand Jerusalem is described as killing the prophets
and stoning those sent there, while on the other hand Jesus
speaks of wishing to gather its children together as a hen
does her chicks. It concludes with the almost contradictory
double message of Jerusalem being 'forsaken and desolate',
and yet also being the place that would greet Jesus with the
words 'Blessed is he who comes in the name of the Lord'. It
is as though the theme of betrayal is applied to Jerusalem
itself: betrayed by its people it becomes forsaken and
desolate rather than the flourishing place of the worship
and service of God. This verse not only echoes the earlier
history of Jerusalem but also its later destiny when its temple was destroyed in AD 70, decades after the death of

Jesus. But there is also another aspect of betrayal related to Jerusalem if the event now associated with Palm Sunday and its greeting, 'Blessed is he who comes in the name of the Lord', is contrasted with the subsequent cries of the Jerusalem crowd to 'Crucify him'. Welcome is turned into rejection.

Certainly the Gospel writers frame Jerusalem as a special place as far as Jesus was concerned, most especially Luke. It was towards Jerusalem that Jesus firmly 'set his face'; it was his place of destiny where he saw his life and its purpose coming to fulfilment. For Luke, as indeed for the Acts of the Apostles, Jerusalem is profoundly important. Not only is it the goal of the journey of Jesus as he moves ever deeper into his Passion, and not only is it the place of his death and final rejection, but it is also the place where the disciples regroup, are transformed and become an outward moving force, taking both the message and the community of God's love into the ever widening world beyond. But all that lies far ahead and well beyond the scope of this book where our concern remains with Jesus, his disciples and those others whose passions filled the Jerusalem of their day. For Luke, certainly, there was feeling enough associated with this place. As part of Jesus' entry to Jerusalem, just before the episode of the cleansing of the temple, Luke describes Jesus as seeing the city and weeping over it (Luke 19:41). In that weeping over Jerusalem we are already well into the Passion of Jesus of Nazareth and are close to what one scholar calls the 'suffering secret' that underlies Luke's Gospel (Marshall 1978: 393).

Temple and Temples

Once in Jerusalem, Matthew, Mark and Luke all tell of Jesus going to the temple and driving from it those who changed the place that should focus on God to a place of human business. But all three of these Gospels set this act – traditionally called the cleansing of the temple – at the end of Jesus' ministry. John, by sharp contrast, places the event at its beginning. In John 2, just after the miracle of water becoming wine at Cana in Galilee, Jesus goes up to Jerusalem and within the context of a Passover, he makes his whip and drives out the traders (John 2:13–22). This is a very good example of the way in which Gospel writers take an event and use it within the overall purpose of their Gospel. It provides a good lesson in biblical studies in encouraging us to look for the significance of the way something is used rather than, for example, trying to make it harmonize in some hard and fast way with the timescale of the other Gospels. John's purpose is very clear because he links the physical temple at Jerusalem with the actual physical body of Jesus (2:20). He argues that the physical temple might have taken 46 years to build but when the temple of Jesus' body is destroyed it will be rebuilt in three days. John writes in a figurative sense to speak of this action as a sign of who Jesus was, for those with eyes to see it. He likens the Resurrection to rebuilding and, in so doing, he introduces into his Gospel the linked theme of resurrection and new life in Christ. Mark's Gospel takes this saying about temples and bodies and places it towards the end of Christ's Passion; indeed, it is used as a testimony against Jesus when he is brought to trial before the high priest. 'We heard him say, "I will destroy this temple that is made with hands, and in three days I will build another, not made with hands"' (Mark 14:58). Mark develops this, though. Instead of just saying, as Matthew and Luke more or less do, that 'My house shall be called a house of prayer', he goes further to describe it as a house of prayer 'for all the nations' (Mark 11:17). One theologian sees this openness for all as the very essence of 'what Jesus' Passion means to Mark' (Schweizer 1971: 236). That would, of course, help to make sense of the alternative ending (Mark 16:9–19) that is included only by some Bibles and which includes the message of Christ to his disciples to preach to the whole creation.

However we interpret this event of Jesus in the temple it was obviously significant for early Christian traditions. This is perfectly understandable because, by the time the Gospels were written, early Christian congregations had, in all probability, not only drawn away from Judaism into their own groups, but were also coming to terms with the fact that the temple at Jerusalem had been destroyed in AD 70. Jewish Christians, in particular, had to rethink all that their Jewish faith and practice had ingrained in them concerning the temple as the central place where God was to be worshipped. The *Letter to the Hebrews* in the New Testament is the best example of how they started thinking through the consequences of the destroyed temple for their own faith. We have already seen the attitude that identified Jesus himself as a kind of temple. Another view, one expressed in the *Letter to the Hebrews*, thought of God's temple as existing in a spiritual way and located in heaven. Yet another approach was to say that the body of each believer was a temple, a place made sacred by the presence of God's Holy Spirit.

Other interpretations are also possible and show how the Christian faith can make numerous patterns of deep religious significance from a particular event. Let me take one, final, example of the cleansing of the temple, from one

of the great artists of the world, Domenicos Theotoco-
poulos. Generally known as 'El Greco' or 'the Greek'
because he was born in Crete he, nevertheless, spent much
of his artistic life in Spain, at Toledo, where he died in
1614. One of his remarkable paintings, to be seen at
London's National Gallery, is called *The Cleansing of the
Temple* and was painted in the late 1580s or early 1590s.
Jesus stands in the middle of the picture in a bustling
corner of the temple. He holds a rope in his right hand and
a toppled table lies before him. He is obviously causing
disruption and a stir. But the real fascination of this piece
lies in what looks like a painting within the painting. At the
top left-hand corner, on what looks like a wall-painting in
the temple – not that it is likely that there ever would have
been such illustrations in Jerusalem's temple – there is a
representation of Adam and Eve being driven out of the
Garden of Eden by an angel.

Here El Greco provides a biblical commentary upon the
New Testament story. Just as sinful Adam and Eve are
driven from God's good garden so sinful men and women
are driven from God's good temple. While the angel in the
mini-picture looks very supernatural and mysterious, Jesus
is painted as a real flesh-and-blood character. This scene
echoes something of our own interpretation in this book.
Jesus had set out on his journey to Jerusalem. He arrived at
his destined place to find even the temple full of that kind
of human business that is blind to the real significance of
life and of God as its ultimate goal. Here was another kind
of betrayal, one that reflects the deepest of Old Testament
themes, in which God's Covenant, God's set of agreements
and formal relationships with humanity, is abandoned and
corrupted through disobedience.

In symbolic terms, Adam and Eve had been given so
much and so little was asked of them, yet they failed. God's

covenant people had been given so much and they failed and, then, the disciples and others encountering Jesus were also given so many opportunities for religious benefit and yet they, too, failed. Once we look at this temple scene of Jesus against the back-cloth of Paradise and with an eye to the underlying current of betrayal then a whole new light is cast on human disobedience. It is not just human curiosity or weakness that emerges but that more personal dimension of spite and hurt that is so often involved in relationships. In other words, we find nothing in this episode of the cleansing of the temple that we will not find in the other events of the Passion of Jesus. People betray the highest goals in the very temple of God just as his disciples will, even more dramatically, betray him before many days are past.

3

The Passions of Peter and Pilate

We are now beginning to see how rejection, denial, betrayal and judgement are closely connected ideas running through the Passion of Christ. These vary only in degree for each individual appearing in the Gospel narrative. In this chapter it is Peter and his denial and Pilate and his judgement of Christ that come to centre stage. While their quite different relationships with Jesus portray the more personal and more public dimensions of Christ's Passion they still show how the elements of the cluster of betrayal interlink with each other and touch upon the themes of faith underlying the Gospel narratives.

Peter's Passion

Peter is among the very first Jesus called to follow him. Along with the other eleven he is with Jesus throughout what looks like the first half of the Gospel story, which is, very largely, filled with miracles and wonders. These serve to illustrate the basic message announced by Jesus, that the Kingdom of God was at hand and that people should repent and believe (Mark 1:15). Just what it was that they should believe is far from easy to discover. Even the parables which talk about this truth in terms of the Kingdom of God seem to hide as much as they reveal (Mark 4:10–12). Certainly, Jesus was preaching that people should repent, and this would not be a strange idea to his fellow Jews. But he also seemed to identify himself as someone who could forgive sins, and here there was a problem for his peers since Jesus was seeing himself as one with an authority to forgive sins, something they saw as God's own domain (Mark 2:1–12). Here we come close to the crucial fact that it is Jesus himself, and the authority that people quite simply saw in him, that was crucial to his early work. Of course, it might well have been the case that popular ideas of the coming Messiah might also have been brought to bear on Jesus by those with an appropriate perspective. On a broader basis, it is easy for us, some 2000 years later, to read back into the Bible all sorts of doctrines that have come into firm shape over the years and in different churches. But when we read the Gospels, even though they were written after many of the epistles, what we encounter is the central life and actions of Jesus of Nazareth. His character, acts and presence overshadow any doctrine. It is the sheer attractive power that seems to draw people to him. Here is a powerful example of what some sociologists call charisma or charismatic power. This word 'charismatic' when used by the sociologists is not the same word used generally to talk about those Christians who also belong to charismatic groups in their churches, people who believe that the Holy Spirit inspires them with special spiritual gifts (*charismata* in Greek). When I talk about Jesus as having charisma I refer to his own power of attraction, the magnetism of leadership, the capacity to inspire confidence in those who felt impelled to follow him. It is part of that feature people recognized when they talked about him teaching as one with authority.

This is not only crucial for the Gospel story in general but for denial, betrayal and judgement in particular because it is the very charisma of Jesus that both attracted and repelled people. For those who became disciples charisma was part of what attracted them and became the basis of trust and inspiration, but for his enemies it appeared as a competing authority, as a challenge to their own status and power. Charisma often becomes a serious problem for long-established traditions of politicians and priests who dislike the personal influence that unique individuals come to exert over people at large – this was also the case for Jesus.

Double Name

So it is we turn to Peter, called by Jesus to be among his followers. Mark's Gospel is simple and direct. Jesus walks along the seashore, sees Peter and his brother Andrew fishing and tells them to follow him and become fishers of men (Mark 1:17). This, of course, was before Peter's name change and when he was still referred to as Simon. The 'renaming' took place some time later when Jesus is described as going into the hills to pray before calling twelve to become his disciples, with Simon being the first and being renamed Peter (Mark 3:16). This new name, meaning a rock, is taken in Matthew's Gospel to indicate that he is a kind of foundation for the emerging church, a natural outcrop that is an obvious basis for building to last (Matthew 16:18). This is, in many respects, a remarkable renaming. It would have been one thing to give a man the name of a rock if his whole life and character indicated an unswerving stability, especially under pressure. But in the very section where the renaming occurs, following his identifying of Jesus as the Messiah, Peter rebukes Jesus and is, in turn, rebuked by him with the 'Get behind me Satan' formula. On the same basis we might expect such a granite figure to stand alongside the one whom he believes to be the Christ and to die with him if necessary. Here Mark's

Gospel *is* quite remarkable for, later in its account, when it comes to the central part of Christ's Passion, Jesus tells his disciples that they will all fall away from him and, in that very section where Jesus also tells Peter that he will betray him, Peter boldly replies that, even if all the others flee he will remain: 'If I must die with you, I will not deny you' (Mark 14:31). 'And', the Gospel continues, 'they all said the same.'

Telling the Truth

Mark's Gospel is remarkable in not hiding the fact that people who were to become key leaders among the earliest Christians had experienced periods of profound weakness and failure. Here we find all the wisdom of the hindsight of faith, for the Gospel was written after small Christian communities had begun to flourish under the influence of a sense of Christ's presence with them. They felt a power that had changed people, especially the original disciples. And this is where Peter and his passion come into focus with its astonishing account of his betrayal of Jesus.

Rather than downplay these acts of betrayal, they are made central. Even the irony of Peter's strong affirmations and his subsequent denial is not hidden or ignored but accentuated. But, at this very point, we need to be careful. It would be easy to set up firm oppositions between Peter the man of rock in his affirmations and the man of sand in the time of trial. That is not, I think, what the Gospels are telling us. Rather, they show a man who is, in many respects, rock-like, but who also fails and they know that this is not an ultimate problem. It is not the kind of flaw which, if someone wrote about it in a reference for a person, would be damning. To describe Peter as it does is to say something about the very life of faith itself. It was part of his rock-like nature that led him to follow the arresting party, at a distance, to see what would happen. He could also have got himself away from the courtyard in which his identity was questioned and which brought him, ultimately, to deny Jesus. Peter's passion was a passion of following Jesus. There was great commitment in it and it was only, as it were, the constant dripping that wore away the stone. It was the interrogation by ordinary people in that courtyard that brought him to deny Jesus. But this was not simply a denial of Jesus, it was also a denial of himself, of a self that only half understood the message of the Kingdom. At least this is something we can say with the wisdom of hindsight, a privilege unavailable to Peter. This is one aspect of Peter's passion that should not be overlooked for it brings into sharp focus the way in which our ideas link up with our experiences. When he denied Jesus it was more despite himself than because of himself. And Peter wept when he did so (Mark 14:72).

That weeping was linked to Peter as the rock. It hints not only at the fact that Simon Peter was magnetically attracted to Jesus but that there must have been something about him that led Jesus to take him into the inner circle of disciples. That 'something' may well have lain behind the famous occasion when Jesus asks his disciples who people think he is, and who they think he is. In response Peter comes out with the affirmation: 'You are the Christ' (Mark 8:29). As we have already seen, this is a crucial moment in these Gospels. So far Jesus has been viewed, very largely, as a miracle worker but now, once this identity is voiced, the message shifts and the element of suffering, judgement and loss is introduced. And it is at this point that Peter rebels. The idea that Jesus should be subjected to rejection and death at the hands of the religious authorities makes Peter rebuke Jesus. Immediately Jesus responds with the famous phrase, 'Get behind me Satan!'(Mark 8:33), and explains that Peter is not on the side of God but of men.

Career Path of Disciples

It is at this point, then, that the issue of discipleship and of following after Jesus begins to become pointed and the question of the nature of the allegiance of the disciples comes to the fore. In clear terms Jesus spells out the nature of discipleship. It means carrying your own cross and losing your life rather than saving it. Here, again, we find one of the most poignant of all of Jesus' sayings: 'For what will it profit a man to gain the whole world and lose his life?' The teaching of Jesus raises serious questions about how we see ourselves and value ourselves and what we have as our goals and motivations.

The double event of Peter's confession and rebuke marks the first step in his denial of Jesus. His vision of Jesus embraced a different career path than one suggested by suffering and death: this was not part of Peter's idea of what the Messiah would be and do. It must have been both confounding and amazing to him as he sought to under-stand what was going on in Jesus' life and mind. To have been so apparently correct about Jesus as the Messiah and then so wrong as to what lay before Jesus could hardly have made Peter's life easy. But he remained with Jesus, reflecting that rock-like aspect of his nature. He is there with him on the night of his arrest in Gethsemane; he is not only there but he acts to defend Jesus. Just as he had once said that 'this should never happen' to Jesus so, when the time arrived, Peter sought to defend his master so that it should not happen to him. It is as though his earlier mis-understanding of the goal of Jesus' ministry had remained with him, lying behind his defensive stroke in cutting off the ear of one of the assailants. This violent act was also, in its own way, a denial of how Jesus was going about his ministry in his final earthly hours.

Then, once more, Mark's Gospel reinforces the idea of suffering in another prediction where Jesus tells his disciples that the Son of Man will be delivered into the hands of wicked men. This time Peter does not rebuke Jesus. It is not that he has learned the true significance of such suffering but simply that he and the others 'did not understand the saying and were afraid to ask him' (Mark 9:31–32). What is obvious is that Mark is making it absolutely clear that suffering is of the essence of Jesus' destiny. That theme is firmly emphasized twice. Then, in the description of Peter's explicit denial of Jesus, the threefold denial hammers home, once more, the denial theme (Mark 14:66–72). In practical terms the whole issue of denial occupies a great deal of space in Mark's Gospel as it does in the Synoptic Gospels at large and, also, in John's Gospel. It is quite obvious that this was a subject of some importance among the earliest Christians, as we shall also see later for Paul.

The Reminder

There is one more episode in Peter's passion that we should recall, though we need to go to John's Gospel for it and to John's very last chapter. There we are given a mysterious account of a resurrection appearance in which Jesus meets Simon Peter, as he is named, when he is out fishing with some of the disciples. They haul in a great catch and arrive at shore to find a figure there who has prepared breakfast for them. They intuitively know that it is Jesus, though the text is odd in saying that none of the disciples dared ask him who he was. Jesus then asks Peter three times whether he loves him. Peter replies that he does, and is told to look

after Christ's flock. But we are told that Peter was grieved
when asked the third time whether or not he loved Christ.
Many a commentator has seen in these three questions an
echo of the earlier threefold denial of Peter. At the end of
that pastoral conversation the command comes to 'follow
me'. It is repeated twice (John 21:19, 22). With that we are
brought back to the sharp focus on following Christ,
brought back to the journey on which he set his course and
which brought him to Jerusalem and to his death. But in
this odd final chapter of John's Gospel, which speaks of the
disciples after the resurrection, the journey continues. We
have an interesting echo of Peter's own life development
when, in one of his speeches in the Acts of the Apostles, he
plainly describes his fellow Jews to themselves as people
who had 'denied the Holy and Righteous One'. That was
when they asked Pilate to release Barabbas and crucify
Jesus, though Peter adds the telling phrase that he knows
they 'acted in ignorance' (Acts 3:17). It is as though the
element of Peter's own ignorance of the need for Christ to
suffer is reflected, on the larger scene, in the Jews at large
not accepting Jesus as the Messiah who had to suffer. The
speech seems to set Peter's experience alongside that of his
compatriots and gives him a degree of understanding of
their situation. A much sharper accusation of betrayal
comes from the closing speech of Stephen just before he
was stoned to death, when he also accuses the religious
authorities of betraying and murdering the Righteous One
(Acts 7:53).

Peter's Real Conversion

When we approach the story of Peter's denial of Jesus we
are often put into a particular frame of mind by the word
'denial'; indeed we speak very readily of Peter's denial. If

we think again about it, focusing on Peter's actions rather than his words, a slightly different perspective emerges. If Peter had, initially, been at a distance from Jesus as far as understanding his true mission was concerned, he was now once more at a distance when Jesus came to his trial. Now it was a physical distance: it was night and it was dark. But he was there. It would be a fateful night, one he was hardly likely to forget; a night of betrayal.

The distance between Peter and the heart of Jesus' message would not be reduced for some time yet. Not, in fact, until after Christ's death and Resurrection, and not until that episode recounted in the Acts of the Apostles when he had a vision of creatures contained in a sheet let down from heaven (Acts 10:9–16). On that day, when he was on a flat housetop waiting for a meal to be prepared, he dreamed of various creatures let down from heaven and was told to kill and eat them. That voice posed a problem. It told him to eat what Jewish law and custom did not allow to be eaten. How could Peter break religious and social customs by eating these animals? This, itself, involved a form of denial. If he ate these things he would be denying his religious upbringing and his understanding of day-to-day Jewish life. It was in the middle of this confusion that understanding came to him. He saw, he understood, that whatever God regarded as true and right was true and right. In practical terms this meant that people who were not Jews were in actual fact of equal standing and worth in God's sight and purposes. This was the major breakthrough of the early Christian community. Anyone and everyone could belong to it, be accepted within it and supported by it. Anyone could find salvation within its fellowship.

But, for the moment, not on the rooftop but in the dark courtyard, Peter watched as the one who would cause this new accepting community to be born was, himself, rejected. That message of the Kingdom of God, so foundational to the teachings of Jesus, was the same message that had brought Jesus to judgement and had brought Peter into the courtyard of his own passion. For Peter was, here and now, still only halfway to that later grasp of the Christian message. Ironically, the man he said he did not know would be the cause of his knowing very many other men and women, not least those coming from beyond his own small world. In that sense he was still not 'converted' to Christianity. In the meantime, and unaware of all that would follow, he had to cope with life as best he understood it. And it looks as though he does not make much sense of what is happening to Jesus and to himself. Why had things come to this? So much had seemed so promising earlier on when he was with Jesus. There was possibility and hope, and now it has all come to nothing.

So when the young woman, the servant-girl, says that she is sure Peter was one of Jesus' disciples he replies, 'Woman, I don't know the man.' Here there is a double statement: a lie and a truth. Of course he lies in his denial of Jesus. But he also speaks the truth: he does not know the man. He does not know the half of him, of what is going on, and of what yet lies ahead. Peter's passion is one of confusion, of a story half told, of a life half lived. When Peter hears the cockerel crowing, he remembers what Jesus said to him about betrayal, and weeps. He weeps not only because of Christ but also for himself.

Pilate's Passion

In turning from Peter to Pilate we seem to enter another world but, as we will see, this appearance soon turns out to be deceptive. Mark's Gospel tells the story of Pilate simply and directly. After Jesus is betrayed he is taken to the high priest and, after being accused of blasphemy as well as denied by Peter, he is taken to Pilate (Mark 15:1–15). Pilate is, obviously, a politically alert person used to dealing with issues of many sorts. He sees he has a problem on his hands, thinks of a way around it that is, unfortunately, frustrated by others, and ends by agreeing to the easy solution. It is, very largely, a cut and dried affair. He asks Jesus the key question that has already landed him in trouble with the Jewish authorities – 'Are you the King of the Jews?' – and receives the roundabout answer, 'You have said so!' After that Jesus is silent, so much so that Pilate is said to have wondered at his silence, given the list of accusations brought against him. Pilate reads the situation as one of priestly envy of Jesus and takes a course of action that would get around the political dealings of a small group of highly motivated persons. He decides to put the vote to the public, as part of a custom of freeing a prisoner at a public holiday. But the option of having either Jesus or the imprisoned rebel Barabbas released turns out not to be so simple after all, when the priests 'stir up the crowds' to have the latter freed. Pilate responds to this rabble-rousing with two questions before acceding to popular pressure and sending Jesus on his way to death.

Considering this story in more detail we soon realise that we are confronted by what we might call Pilate's passion of questions. In Mark 14–15 we encounter one of the most condensed sets of questions in the New Testament: 'Are you the King of the Jews?' 'Have you no answer to make?' 'Do you want me to release the King of the Jews?' 'What shall I do with the man?' 'What evil has he done?' (Mark 15:2–12). In John's Gospel the exchange between Jesus and Pilate is quite lengthy and ends with Pilate's question that has echoed down the ages: 'What is truth?' (John

18:38). Matthew, for his part, also contributes to our own popular expression with his equally powerful account of Pilate 'washing his hands' in a literal sense, to rid himself of responsibility. At this point all the people answer, 'His blood be upon us and on our children' (Matthew 27:25). Here the element of judgement stands to the fore and the various accounts make the point that Jesus is innocent and yet is killed, while the guilty criminal Barabbas is set free. Pilate knew that envy was at the heart of the false accusations against Jesus and yet he, too, finally goes with the voice of popular demand and hands Jesus over for crucifixion (Matthew 27:18). In John's Gospel there is a sense that Pilate really did want to release Jesus but that the pressure of public opinion was too strong so that he capitulated (John 19:12). Even so, in terms of the pattern we see emerging in the Passion of Jesus, Pilate now takes his place with those who had some insight into the situation of Jesus but who did not follow his better judgement. Rather like the rich young ruler he goes his own way as part of the abandonment of Jesus.

Pilate, the governor under Roman authority, is one of the numerous characters regarded as part of the dark plot against Jesus as far as many readers of the Bible are concerned. We look at him and see a weak man. We find him guilty as we judge him through his judging of Jesus. But in pondering Pilate's predicament we begin to observe some elements of that passion common to many of our lives, common to many human situations where complexity meets uncertainty, and where the opinions of others press heavily upon us. In the Gospels Pilate comes to be the focus for the great issues, for the questions that have surrounded Jesus and his journey to Jerusalem. The ideas that the disciples entertained, half-understood and sometimes fervently desired, come to a head in the issue of Jesus and his identity. What had largely been implicit now becomes explicit and judgement is passed upon it. Two of Pilate's utterances demand some final comment: the question, 'What is truth?', and his words when presenting Christ to the people, 'Behold the man'.

What is Truth?

This question of Pilate in John's Gospel has played its own key part in the lives of millions of people ever since, with some becoming followers of Christ and some not. Certainly, it is no easy question, not least because of the varied pictures of Jesus presented by different churches. Sometimes we hear the crisp and official answers of a church but then go on to wonder just what they mean. The image comes to mind of the question Jesus put to his hearers one day when he asked them if it is easier to say 'pick up your bed and walk' or to say 'your sins are forgiven'. The obvious answer was that it is easier to say 'your sins are forgiven' – for there is no obvious test of that – than to tell a long-term invalid to walk. So it is with the identity of Jesus for, while it is easy to say that Jesus is Lord, or that he is the Son of God, it is not always easy so to grasp his significance that we can turn it into a life that displays the Kingdom.

For many, the life of faith is far from simple and a great many of us know it. There are times when individuals find it is easy to agree with religious doctrines and there are times when they can hardly see the way ahead at all. There are some people who find faith easy but there are many more for whom the great questions find only occasional answers here and there. This is one reason why Pilate's passion can echo within our own experience when questions seem to be the only way of addressing ourselves to God.

When it comes to answers there are many, today, who speak of the postmodern world as a kind of attitude of mind surrounding the way we live. By this they mean that there are many different answers to questions and that there is no certainty to be found anywhere. Each person lives as he or she wills and nobody should contradict them. There is no shared set of values and beliefs by which all may live. In each town there is a mix of cultures and of values and each is expected to respect all others. There is, it seems to me, a great deal of truth in this picture and it presents a challenge for Christians that should not be shrugged off as though it did not matter. It is easy, for example, to dig deep into a kind of fundamentalism and to shout old slogans against the new circumstances. It is also relatively easy to throw the past to the winds as though it never counted for anything. Both are, probably, unwise. One challenge is to see Christian communities of faith not as places where all answers are given but where individuals commit themselves to the life of Jesus of Nazareth and to see what happens in the process, allowing working solutions to emerge from lived experience. For churches are communities in which believers, be they strong or weak in faith, be they betraying or betrayed, can point and say 'behold the man'.

Behold the Man

These words come in John's Gospel after Jesus has been judged, scourged, given a crown of thorns (struck by the soldiers as they mockingly called him 'the King of the Jews') and dressed in a mock royal robe. Pilate brings him out to the people, while actually affirming that he finds no fault in him, and says, 'Behold the man' (John 19:5). The response was immediate with the popular cry, 'Crucify him!'

'Behold the man'. Certainly it could not be doubted
that he was a man, while his mock royal robe and crown
begged the question of the claims made against him. This
statement is, itself, as much of a question as any of the
actual questions in Pilate's passion. Jesus, the man from
Galilee, has been and will, doubtless, continue to be a
question standing before the lives of individuals and
societies.

Never was this more clearly and dramatically seen
than in July 1999 when a statue of Christ was placed in
Trafalgar Square, London, for a six-month period. It completed a plinth that had been built in 1834 for some national
hero, but had remained unoccupied for over a century and
a half. Something of a national debate led to this life-size
figure being the first of a changing series of exhibits topping
that pillar. The sculptor, Mark Wallinger, called the piece
Ecce Homo, the Latin version of Pilate's words, 'Behold
the man'. Of course, this was just a statue. But statues tell
us much about the age that produces and admires them.
The six-foot figure stood with hands tied behind its back
and with a crown of thorns on its head. The body was
slightly asymmetrical and the face expressionless. It was
very ordinary. The most extraordinary thing about this
sculpture was the company it kept so high above the
milling crowds of tourists. Apart from Lord Nelson atop
his famous column in the centre there are three others
making up the square. These include King George IV,
Major General Sir Henry Havelock and General Charles
Napier. These three are royally or militarily dressed with
George on horseback and with Napier sword in hand. The
Christ figure was completely out of place. This made his
powerlessness obvious, and did so in a context of the might
of a nation. The one historical figure it did seem to echo
was that of Mahatma Gandhi, the man whose ideology of

passive non-resistance would ultimately help free India from the power of Imperial Britain in 1947.

With Pilate, then, as with Peter, we find the cluster of betrayal reflected in mixed emotions and conflicting attitudes. The accounts given of them are direct and serve as a most appropriate frame for turning to Judas, the one who normally is made to carry the load of betrayal largely by himself.

4

The Passion of Judas

There are not many names that trigger as powerful a negative response as that of Judas, and none of us would ever wish to be called Judas! It would be too shameful and, as with many shameful things, we instinctively pass over them as soon as they come to mind. Yet here in Judas, as long-standing a disciple of Jesus as any of the rest, is one whose own passion deserves our attention. He was one the disciples must have trusted since, as John's Gospel tells us, they had given him the task of looking after their money. But today he is the man none of us trusts. His very name holds poison and stands for all that is at enmity with friendship. Not only do we normally give him no second thought, but he is positively absent from our mind. Seldom would a sermon be preached on him. He has been abolished. Judas is an obvious case to study in relation to the cluster of betrayal that features throughout this book. Indeed, his betrayal would be expected to be at its very centre, and so it is. But the very fact that we have identified what we have called a cluster of betrayal indicates that he should not be a sole figure, isolated from all others. That is why this book sets others alongside him, all responsible to some degree for an aspect of rejecting Jesus.

When Judas is given any thought at all it is usually his act of betrayal that comes to the fore with the other aspects of his life being ignored. This is a pity since Matthew's Gospel also tells how Judas both repented and killed himself (Matthew 27:3–10). For Judas underwent suffering of a kind hard for us to imagine in those dramatic days surrounding the Passover. For him, as for Jesus, the Passover ended in death: for both of them death was part of what they had lived for, even though their motives and the way they met their end may have been so very different.

Judas and the Gospels

Judas is much more woven into the Gospel accounts of the Passion of Christ than we often appreciate. All three Synoptic Gospels and the Gospel of John tell the combined story of betrayal and kiss. For Mark it is the simple account that while Jesus was eating the Passover meal with his disciples he indicates that one of them will betray him, and adds the sad warning, 'Woe to the man by whom he is betrayed' (Mark 14:18). Matthew pinpoints Judas as one who asks Jesus, 'Is it I?', with Jesus replying, 'You have said so' (Matthew 26:25). John resembles Mark by stressing the fact that they were all eating together, but adds the poignant image of Jesus actually handing some food to Judas. John then adds the telling commentary that 'after the morsel Satan entered', and Judas immediately left the band of disciples (John 13:27, 30).

For John's Gospel this is a terrible moment, for Judas does not simply leave: he goes out into the night. The phrase, 'and it was night', rings in our ears for this Gospel is full of the shades of good and evil. Its opening verses proclaim that 'the light shines in the darkness, and the darkness has not overcome it' (John 1:5). It describes human beings as loving 'darkness rather than light' (John 3:19). It claims that Jesus is the 'light of the world' and that those who follow him 'will not walk in darkness but will have the light of life' (John 8:12). At his moment of leaving the Passover meal Judas was walking precisely into that kind of darkness that is death and that ended in his own death. Unlike Nicodemus, the religious teacher and seeker who came in out of the night to speak to Jesus and to seek the truth, Judas moves in the opposite direction.

We can but guess at his motives. Some have thought of Judas as one who believed deeply that Jesus was the Messiah, who really would deliver the people from their enemies, and that what was needed was some trigger to make Jesus reveal his real identity and to bring about God's just rule. His arrest would certainly be such a critical moment. For others it was an act of simple greed following Matthew's account that tells of Judas going to the chief priests and asking how much they will give him to betray Jesus (Matthew 26:14). In John's Gospel there is a clear assertion that Judas 'was a thief' and used to steal from the disciples' funds (John 12:6). The context in which Judas went out to betray Jesus in Matthew's narrative is just as telling as John's cameo of Judas going out into the night. Matthew places Judas' exit in the context of the story of the woman who anoints Jesus with 'very expensive oint-ment' as a kind of preparation for his death. Was it that Judas simply did not like to see the waste and would have preferred to get his hands on the money, or was it that not until then did he realise how serious Jesus was about his destiny with death? Was he simply a self-interested thief, or was it that he came to see something of the implication of Jesus and his message and did not want to be part of it? We can never know the answer to these questions. It is better, perhaps, to ask just what it was that Judas betrayed. To that poignant issue we devote ourselves in a later chapter. For the moment we simply note John's view that the under-lying betrayal is as fundamentally evil as it can be, in that the devil is the source of Judas' betraying Jesus (John 13:2). What is obvious is that betrayal is profoundly central to John's Gospel, as to the other three Gospels, and that for John it is of the essence of evil for it breaks up the oneness and unity of the disciples with Christ. As far as John is concerned it is just such a unity that marks the divine fellowship, whether between the Father and Son or between Jesus and his disciples. The keynote of John's Gospel on this issue lies in the prayer of Christ that all believers 'might be one' (John 17:21), including those who would come to faith through the preaching of the disciples. It is of obvious concern to John's Gospel that Judas had spoiled this unity for, in chapter 17, often described as Jesus' prayer for the Church or his high priestly prayer, he refers to the fact that none has been lost 'except the son of perdition' (John 17:12).

As the story proceeds, it becomes obvious that betrayal is also profoundly evil as far as Judas himself is concerned. Matthew tells us that when Judas realised that Jesus 'was condemned he repented and brought back the thirty pieces of silver' to the authorities, telling them that he had 'betrayed innocent blood'. They, however, refuse to accept it and tell him to sort out his own problems by himself (Matthew 27:3). Judas does just this by flinging down the coins in the temple and going out and hanging himself. Matthew ensures that we do not miss the depth of Judas' regret, both by recording that Judas had repented and by noting his words to the authorities, 'I have sinned' (Matthew 27:3, 4). There is a deep significance in this moment of Matthew's Gospel because Judas comes to be one of the judges of Jesus. He judges him to be an innocent man just before he is taken for his trial before the governor. In fact Matthew lines up a series of 'informal judges' for Jesus: the governor's wife who has a dream about 'that righteous man'; the crowd who prefer the convicted criminal Barabbas; the guards who mock him as 'King of the Jews'; his fellow victims of crucifixion who 'revile him'; and a centurion standing at the cross who describes Jesus to be 'truly the Son of God' (Matthew 27:19, 23, 29, 54). Here we are presented with a spectrum of opinion, as if to show just how difficult the governor's final decision would be in due course.

The First Christian?

But what of Judas? Are we, perhaps, to view him as the first Christian? The first to anticipate and see something of the one he had betrayed and, in the light of that, to repent and to know the pressure of sin? Perhaps that is to take things too far in terms of Matthew's Gospel, which does not interpret the death of Jesus in strong terms of sacrifice for sin but as vindicating his identity as the King of the Jews through the Resurrection. It would be equally possible to speak of Judas as a man who knows the pressure of sin and the need of repentance but who awaits that saviour from sin, the one who yet has to suffer, be vindicated and come to bring life to the disciples.

For us, however, Judas' death does bring something of the tragedy of life into sharp focus. Here was an individual whose life had become caught up in the life of a great man. Together they had experienced public and private events; his life had been made more exciting and challenging than it would probably ever have been had he not met Jesus. He had come to have dealings with people in positions of authority, and now it had all come to nothing. So much might have happened: there had been so many possibilities, but now there was only despair. All that he had come to live for, or at least to ponder and relate to his own life, had come crashing down around him, and it seemed his own fault. If he had made an error of judgement in trying to force Jesus' hand to disclose himself as Messiah, that had gone wrong. Certainly, whatever friendship had existed between them had turned to regret and bitterness.

This very issue of life coming to nothing frames the passion of Judas: so much coming to so little. This is one reason why his story is so easily or intentionally ignored. When we read the Gospels we look to find significance, meaning and a positive purpose in their parables and accounts of what Jesus and others did. Hope and anticipation, expectation and a degree of optimism surround us. Against that background Judas stands almost as a solitary figure. I say almost because of that young man discussed earlier who eagerly runs up to Jesus to find out how best to live, and is told to give away what he has and to follow Jesus. The answer is too much for him and he 'went away sorrowful for he had great possessions' (Matthew 19:16–22). The extreme case of Judas and the lesser case of the rich young man both highlight the way Jesus had set for himself and the path that disciples were expected to tread, but from which these two had deviated.

The Greeting

It was with a kiss of greeting that Judas took his departure on the way of perdition. Matthew's account is particularly poignant on this as it portrays Judas greeting Jesus with 'hail Master!', only to be greeted in return when Jesus calls him 'friend' and asks, 'Why are you here?' (Matthew 26:49, 50). The customary address of 'Master' or 'Rabbi' marked the relationship that had embraced them both for the last few years, a relationship underscored by the word 'friend'. It was from the midst of friendship that Jesus was

betrayed, from a friendship born of close proximity and
fostered by a degree of mutual commitment that must have
been more than transient. This is one reason why the
betrayal is all the more galling and easily reminds us of the
psalmist speaking of betrayal as coming 'even from mine
own familiar friend in whom I trusted' (Psalm 41:9). Or,
again, Psalm 55 speaks of one who taunts him and says
that he could have borne it had this come from an enemy
but, to come from a friend, was too devastating (vv. 12,
13). But this is precisely the situation in which Jesus is
betrayed with that kiss of friendship. Such is the very stuff
of the Gospel as it shows the personal relationships in
and through which Jesus sought to work. Whatever his
message of the Kingdom was, it certainly involved friendship and close co-operation and it was just that closeness of
shared purpose that Judas had contradicted. Tragedy
frames this failure.

Moreover, theirs is a story not far removed from our
own lives. Whether at the extreme or more limited end we
encounter a failure of nerve in ourselves or in those we
know and love. We know the paths that should have been
followed and were missed and, most especially, the friend-
ships that have been ruptured through our own misdoing.
Then if something terrible happens, as when suicide strad-
dles our path, we are often at a loss to know just what
caused it. We examine events and pressures, crises and
personal histories, all so that we may be able to escape the
profundity of someone taking their own life. If only we
knew the answer then, somehow, we feel the pain would be
eased a little. But this is not entirely satisfactory, indeed
it is seldom possible to achieve, for there is a degree of
opacity of one person to another that makes our knowledge of each other distinctly imperfect. We know so little
about other people, about what motivates them or lies in

their experience and memory. Indeed, it may be that many people know only a little about themselves. And what if that was also true of Judas? What if he was clear about some aspects of his life as a disciple of Jesus and quite confused or even unaware of others? Is that something we are prepared to allow him? Perhaps it should be, since it is not obvious that we should expect Judas to be so very much clearer about his life and actions than the other disciples or, indeed, ourselves.

The Kiss of Death

But perhaps the point is that we want Judas to be sure of things. We want him to be purely evil so that we can draw a sharp distinction between him and the other disciples and between him and ourselves. The moment we are prepared to see him, at least in some way, as similar to ourselves a danger signal begins to flash. So much seems to circle around that kiss of betrayal. Even though our culture finds kissing a difficult custom among people other than family and, perhaps, relatively close friends, we find the idea of this kiss of Judas deeply distressing. The very words of Luke's text seem to strike home with their devastating message: 'The man called Judas, one of the twelve . . . drew near to Jesus to kiss him' (Luke 22:47). Jesus is said to have asked Judas if he would betray him with a kiss. This highlights the betrayal. It makes the whole process explicit and conscious and makes this kiss of death all the more obvious. A sign of love, of respect of the disciple for his master, is turned into a symbol of hate. It is the very thought of intimacy and closeness that makes betrayal what it is, a turning away from the purposes of the one we love. It is abandonment. But it is also a separation of ourselves from part of ourselves. This, perhaps, is why

Judas goes and hangs himself for, not only has he turned against Jesus but, in so doing, he has turned against part of himself. It was no wonder the world crashed around Judas, for part of himself had been caused to vanish.

In what was once a very well-known and influential Christian poem entitled 'The Hound of Heaven', published in 1893, Francis Thompson describes how God pursues individuals to love and to win them over despite themselves. The poet looks back on his life and sees how he had sought to escape the divine lover, all to no avail, for he was finally overtaken and overwhelmed by love.

> I fled Him, down the nights
> > And down the days;
> I fled Him, down the arches
> > Of the years;
> I fled Him, down the labyrinthine
> > Ways
> Of my own mind: and in the
> > Midst of tears
> I hid from Him, and under running
> > Laughter.

Then he describes how he sensed God in the chase and became increasingly aware of 'those strong Feet, that followed, followed after'.

> > But with unhurrying chase,
> > And unperturbed pace,
> Deliberate speed, majestic instancy,
> > They beat – and a Voice beat
> > More instant than the Feet –
> 'All things betray thee, who betrayest Me'.

Here he highlights the truth of the double-edged nature of betrayal: 'All things betray thee, who betrayest Me'.

Francis Thompson knew the power of betrayal. He speaks of trying to tempt those who were faithful to God only to find,

> My own betrayal in their constancy.
> In faith to Him their fickleness to me,
> Their traitorous trueness, and their loyal deceit.

This whole poem touches on the heart of the passions of the disciples described in this book and has also touched the lives of many subsequent Christians. Even by 1928 that poem had already sold 225 thousand copies. This simple statistic is, in its own way, a measure of popular faith, for the poem itself is rather complicated and yet, even when the words are not very clear, the powerful sense of what it means comes through, conveying the image of life's complexities and the divine presence.

Judas, too, had a life embroiled in complexity. As we look back on the biblical story it seems all too obvious that Jesus was working out a life of insight into God's will and of obedience to it and we may wonder why Judas could not see that. We think that, as a disciple of Jesus, his privileged position should have given him easy access into God's ways and purposes. But that was not the case, as we also see in our exploration of Peter's passion. It was not until after the Crucifixion that Peter came to see the power of God working through Jesus' life and opening up divine love and purpose to all people, not only Jews. Judas was not granted time for such a realisation to dawn. For him betrayal led rapidly to disappointment, chaos and the decision for suicide. What we cannot escape is the fact that the Passion of Jesus involves the suicidal death of Judas. The narratives suggest the double betrayal involved in this tragic event for Judas in the betrayal of the Master and of himself.

Judas as Myth

It is easy to think of Judas, and his response to Jesus, in terms of the cluster of betrayal also reflected by others in the Gospel stories. To do so shows that Judas was not unique and also provides a different view from those who see in Judas a tradition of Christian anti-Semitism. Some argue that Christians have isolated Judas, as the one really wicked member of the group of disciples, because of a strong spirit of anti-Semitism, and that the very name establishes 'Jewish evil . . . as a universal benchmark for the ages' (Maccoby 1992: 161). This is because Judas, as a name, actually means 'Jew', and some have thought that he stands as a kind of symbol for all Jews as far as a Christian outlook is concerned, even to the point of arguing that he did not actually exist as an individual. It is true that Christians have, at times, taken an anti-Semitic position, one that can be fuelled by some parts of the New Testament (especially the Gospel of John), and this has been reflected in some of the services surrounding the Passion and death of Christ.

But it is also true to say that many Christians see Judas as a symbol of themselves, as those who have betrayed Christ. To take it a step further, there is a depth of Christian spirituality that understands its own weakness and frailty in such a way that it can see the Jews, depicted in the Gospels as denying Christ, as being representatives of anyone and everyone who denies Jesus. In this book we place Judas alongside many others, including contemporary Christians, as one caught up in the cluster of betrayal. It is for that reason that this figure occupies but one chapter in this book, and one that is not emphasized dramatically above any other. This brings him into focus without either ignoring him, as the beginning of this chapter suggested is often done by Christians, or throwing an excessive spotlight upon his moment of betrayal.

5

The Supper

The Last Supper was the meal that brought betrayal into the heart of Christian spirituality. It portrays key features of the cluster of betrayal in relation to the disciples as a group and not only to specific individuals. There are rare moments in life and history when a belief becomes so charged with emotion and so focused on some person, word or event that it is never to be forgotten. The Last Supper was one such moment. What happened there bore deep into the memories of the disciples who went on to become leaders of the Christian congregations of the Mediterranean world, groups out of which would flow the writings that include the Gospels and epistles that now form the New Testament. For us, as for them, memory can become both a treasure and a prison, holding the joys and sorrows of our lives and often influencing our future far more than we appreciate.

The most remarkable demonstration of this influence lies in the fact that today's Christian Churches still hold a service based on that Last Supper Jesus held with his disciples. After 2000 years memories are still prompted and imaginations stimulated by this ceremony whose roots go back to Christ. In fact those roots are much older still, extending into earlier Jewish history as the Passover meal. As a powerful part of Jesus' own Jewish tradition, this ritual occasion now came to be marked in a new way, taking on a new life of its own and becoming one firm foundation for the new Christian Church. While each denomination has added to it and developed it in dramatically different forms it still echoes that founding event when the meaning of life, and the emotion underlying it, was focused on the words and actions of Jesus as a rabbi among his disciples.

At the outset it is worth asking how difficult contemporary Christians might find it to understand the Last Supper as described in the Gospels. There are at least two reasons that make the task difficult. First, because modern ideas of the Last Supper are influenced by people's experience of the Eucharist. Although this ritual possesses a variety of names in different Christian traditions be it the Mass, Lord's Supper, Holy Communion or Sacred Liturgy, it is still an identifiable event. Whatever its name it is a service of deep significance for many people yet remains far removed from what Jesus and his disciples would have known as first-century Jews. Secondly, only a few Christians have a Jewish cultural background and are familiar with the Passover festival.

In this chapter I want to emphasize only one element of the Last Supper: betrayal. This is an extremely powerful feature in the Gospel writings but has become almost entirely lost in the services now held by Christians. Here, above all, we have Jesus bringing betrayal before our very eyes and yet, despite that fact, the theme of betrayal plays an almost insignificant part both in our consideration of the Eucharist and of the history of the faith expressed in doctrine and beliefs.

The Supper's History

The Last Supper held by Jesus and his disciples was almost certainly a Passover meal. It occurred at the time of year of the Passover, a time when each family was required to eat a meal of bitter herbs, unleavened bread, a lamb and wine, to celebrate the ancient delivery of their ancestors out of bondage in Egypt. The name of the event came from the fact that the divine presence had 'passed over' the Jewish families whose houses were marked by blood taken from the slaughtered lambs. But that same divine power resulted in the death of the first-born son of the Egyptians who had, stubbornly, kept the Jews as slave-prisoners and would not let them free. So it was that the Passover was a memorial meal in which members of the family recalled that deliverance, with the youngest child having the task of asking what it all meant. This prompted the story of deliverance wrought by God against his people's enemy. The meal was symbolic of haste and readiness to depart. It was a way of asserting and affirming one's identity as a Jew, one belonging to the people that God had delivered. In terms of the Hebrew scriptures the Passover meal was a meal that initiated the journey of deliverance. To mark their readiness to depart they were to eat it dressed ready to leave, with their walking staffs in their hand. It was the last meal before departing from Egypt.

So it was that the Passover in the time of Jesus would be eaten by families just as a rabbi did with his disciples. It should be eaten at Jerusalem, at the holy city which, despite many turns in its fortune, had come to represent the fulfilment of God's promise to give his people a land of their own. But, as history had determined, Jerusalem had now fallen under the foreign control of Rome. It would only be another generation before its temple, the pride and joy of the Jewish people, would be destroyed. Jesus would have been familiar with the Passover meal from the time when he was a little boy and would, himself, have asked the set questions of what the meal meant. He would have heard many times the tale of God's deliverance. Much as

Christians today hear again the message of Christmas so, then, the boy Jesus would have had a deep familiarity with this gathering together of the family, in the knowledge that their neighbours would be doing likewise.

And now he came to this particular Passover, the one he was to eat with his disciples in that large, upper room that had been booked in advance (Mark 4:12–16). But there is a difference between this Passover and the others he has celebrated for, instead of the emphasis falling on that past deliverance, it now shifts to betrayal and to his death that is, itself, closely linked to the coming Kingdom of God. The message here is strong and deep. Whereas traditional Passovers concerned deliverance, this Last Supper concerned deliverance grounded in betrayal. While the Passover was about a tightly bound family group this meal was marked, indeed marred, by the flaw of a betrayer. Destruction lay within and not outside the household. It is this fact that makes the Last Supper so poignant. As far as Jesus is concerned he awaits not deliverance from destruction but delivery to destruction.

The strong emotion of betrayal is very obvious in Mark's Gospel. It is the very first topic raised by Jesus once they were at the table. 'One of you will betray me, one who is eating with me.' Here the intimacy of this shared meal, not just any meal but the key meal of God's chosen people, is ruptured. The disciples are sorrowful and ask who the betrayer is. Jesus answers that it is one who is sharing in the very food that should unite them as people set within the purposes of God. To eat together is to be together; it marks friendship and closeness, but that very rule of hospitality is now broken by deceit.

In many respects this meal summarizes those earlier moments of shared unity and concern recounted in the Gospels, including that rich young man who had come to

Jesus and gone away sorrowful and the woman who had lavished expensive ointment on him. Here, at last, we might think that Jesus will be among friends; here at least his love will be repaid with love, his friendship with friendship. And so it should have been, but it was not. It is John's Gospel that allows us the greatest insight into this paradox of friendship and betrayal.

John's Supper

This Gospel allows us to pinpoint the heart of the passion of the Last Supper in a distinctive way. John describes Jesus as being 'troubled in spirit' when announcing that one of them would betray him (John 13:21). The image presents Jesus as knowing that one of those who had been so close to him did not wish to be part of the unity of the Master and disciple band, holding love to be the goal and purpose of God's will for humanity. John's Gospel rearranges most of the events that make up what I describe as the passion of the Last Supper and gives them a distinctive emphasis. This is a powerful reminder that different Gospels, letters and books of the Bible often present particular ideas, events or stories in ways that emphasize different truths. Just as some Christians find their faith stimulated by insights that might not appeal to others so it is in the Bible. At first sight this can appear difficult if we expect all biblical passages to say the same thing or if it appears that there are contradictions in the texts. In this case of the Last Supper, for example, there are minor differences between all the Gospels but major ones between the Synoptics and John. In Matthew, for example, Judas asks, 'Is it I, Master?' when the question of betrayal comes up, but this is absent in Mark, while in Luke the disciples question one another about who it might be (Matthew 26:25; Luke 22:23).

These and other differences should not be ignored but fully embraced because they increase our grasp of the motives lying behind the different Gospel writers and the meaning they impart through their accounts. To see the purpose of the writers is to enter into their understanding of events that are hard to exhaust because they touch the depths of life and faith.

In brief the problem is that John's Gospel differs significantly from those of Matthew, Mark and Luke as far as the Last Supper is concerned. As I mentioned in chapter 1 these three Gospels are often called the Synoptic Gospels because they offer a generally similar view of events, and because they are distinguished from John's Gospel which often gives its own distinctive presentation and interpretation of events. A good case in point is when John sets the Last Supper 'before the Feast of the Passover' (John 13:1). He does this for the very particular reason that it allows him to place the Crucifixion of Jesus at the very time when the Passover lambs were being killed in readiness for the Passover meal. In other words, John wants to say that the death of Jesus was to be identified with the killing of the Passover lambs. Jesus was, for John, the lamb of God who takes away the sin of the world just as John the Baptist had announced at the outset of John's Gospel (John 1:29).

How, then, does the Passion of Christ begin to show itself in John's equivalent of the Last Supper? To begin with John simply speaks of a supper and not of the Passover (John 13:2); then, most significantly, he totally avoids any reference to the bread and wine as being Christ's body and blood. He can do this because he has already dealt with this message earlier when arguing that Jesus is 'the bread of life' who gives his flesh to be the life of the world (John 6:35, 51). That same chapter also adds the reference to Christ's blood: 'He who eats my flesh and drinks my blood has eternal life' (John 6:44). In fact that chapter is a most important chapter for us because, at the outset of the teachings of Jesus, John's Gospel introduces the idea of betrayal and the fact that, on hearing this 'hard saying' about Christ being the bread of God coming down from heaven, 'many of his disciples drew back and no longer went about with him' (John 6:66). At that very point Jesus is said to ask his twelve disciples if they, too, wished to go away. More than this, and in the same place where Peter announces that Jesus is the one who has the words of eternal life, Jesus states the fact that he had chosen them and yet one of them 'is a devil'. For, as John's Gospel puts it, he 'spoke of Judas, the son of Simon Iscariot, for he, one of the Twelve, was to betray him' (John 6:66–71).

What is unmistakable both in John 6, the bread of life chapter, and chapter 13, the supper chapter, is the stress on betrayal. The latter, in particular, develops the theme of the close bonds between Jesus and his disciples. It speaks of the disciple whom Jesus loved and of the closeness of the group at the supper, and it is against that background that three main features emerge in John's Last Supper: humble service, betrayal and glory. It is as though betrayal is framed or set off by humility and glory. Humility comes in the account of Jesus washing the disciples' feet (John 13:4–12). This is unique to John, being quite absent in Matthew, Mark and Luke, though each of those three Gospels do record words of Jesus that concern service and humility and the fact that earthly rulers and masters lord it over their people but Christian disciples should not do so (Matthew 20:25–28; Mark 19:42–45; Luke 22:22–24).

John's Gospel is distinctive in the message it lays before us because it looks back with all the wisdom of Christian hindsight and with the eye of faith. It builds up a pattern of Christian truth, a theology of its own, to explain what the

life and death of Jesus meant and how the Christian community, of which this Gospel writer was a part, accepted
Jesus, worshipped and lived for him. In that pattern of belief
in John's Gospel, Jesus is aware that things are coming to a
climax and that the purpose of his life must now be clari-
fied for the disciples. Crucially, the Supper is a time when
the devil has already put it into Judas' heart to betray Jesus
(John 13:2). John emphasizes this by having Jesus say to
the disciples after washing their feet, ' "you are clean, but
not every one of you". For he knew who was to betray him'
(John 13:10). In other words the foot-washing occurs in
the face of betrayal. Judas has also had his feet washed by
the one he, too, has come to call Master and Lord. The act
of foot-washing is followed by the teaching on humility
and mutual service. Then, once more, the issue of betrayal
comes up and a reference is made back to the Old Testament and to a text describing the hostility of someone who
has already enjoyed his friend's hospitality. The fuller text
of that sad Psalm still speaks to us today: 'even my bosom
friend in whom I trusted, who ate my bread, has lifted his
heel against me' (Psalm. 41:9).

It is just here, at the Supper, that Jesus is said by John to
be 'troubled in spirit'. This seems to be the equivalent distress that the other Gospels place after the Supper and in
the Garden of Gethsemane. In John's Gospel, there is no
agony in the garden, no prayer, no sleeping disciples and
no kiss of betrayal (John 18:1–12). Certainly, betrayal is
mentioned and Judas is there, leading the soldiers, but it is
Jesus who takes the lead and offers himself up to them.
This highlights Jesus as taking the initiative as when Peter,
as impulsive as ever, cuts off the ear of one of the arresting
party and Jesus tells him to sheathe his sword and that he
must 'drink the cup which the Father has given me' (John
18:11). All this is quite different from the Synoptic

Gospels. There are elements of the Gethsemane story here, to be sure – the garden, the arrest, the betrayal, Judas, the sword and cut ear, and a question about a cup that must be drunk – but there is no agony, no prayer that the hour might pass and that he might not have to drink the cup lying before him. In John's Gospel it is as though the great divine plan is working itself out and the betrayal of Judas is simply part of that plan.

One reason for dwelling on this distinction between John and the other Gospels is to stress the need not to follow John to the exclusion of the other Gospels, not to emphasize the divine plan to such an extent that we gloss over the accounts of the garden and its agony in Matthew, Mark and Luke. Even the words from the cross detailed in John's Gospel reflect a divine purpose and plan. Jesus ensures that one of his disciples looks after his mother, says 'I thirst' in order to fulfil a scripture, and then announces, 'It is finished' (John 19:26–30). Our stress on Gethsemane will depend more upon the other Gospels as they take us closer to the side of the man from Nazareth whose destiny is not an easy one and whose Passion is not lived to some ideal plan. But, for the moment, we remain with John and with the Last Supper where, after the teaching of humility and the foot-washing, there comes the greatly elaborated conversation on betrayal. His being troubled in spirit is due to his knowledge that one of them will betray him. They all want to know who it is, so Peter asks the beloved disciple, the one closest to Jesus, to ask who it is. And, as we have already described, Jesus passes food to the betrayer. The symbol of friendship immediately triggers a response of enmity. Just as Jesus has already washed that disciple's feet so he now offers him food, yet even the two moments of opportunity fail to release the response of love.

John, with great dramatic power and theological insight,

describes this moment with its underlying power for evil by saying that 'after the morsel, Satan entered into him'. Then Jesus takes control and says to Judas, 'What you are going to do, do quickly' (John 13:27). Judas then leaves straight after eating the food from Jesus' hand and, as John so forcefully expresses it, 'it was night'.

It was night in the physical world of Jerusalem but, much more importantly, it was night in the moral world of Judas. But even that darkness is turned to a positive purpose by John as he moves to the third major element of the Supper: glory. For it is just when Judas has gone out into the dark that 'the Son of man is glorified' (John 13:31). For John the real core group of disciples is now together with Jesus and to this band, to his 'little children', he gives a new commandment: that they should love one another as he had loved them (John 13:34). John's Gospel now adds four whole chapters of teaching about his relationship with God as his Father and of the relationship the disciples will have with that same divine Father due to their faith in Jesus. Here we learn that Jesus is the way, the truth and the life as well as the true vine; that the Spirit will come to lead them in the future because soon they will not see Jesus for some time. Towards the end of these intensely devotional and inspirational addresses Jesus still has to tell the disciples that they will 'all be scattered and will leave me alone' (John 16:32). Alone, that is, except for the Father who remains with him. This is a telling comment because, in John's Gospel, there is no cry from the cross to indicate that Jesus has been forsaken by his heavenly Father.

Here, in John, the Supper has become the means of concentrating teaching on love and unity between believer, Christ and God, a unity in love that is the very nature of glory (John 17:22). Indeed the image of a unified community, one that is not internally divided even though it may be scattered by external attack, constitutes the core concern of this part of John's Gospel. Yet, despite this picture, the text of this Gospel moves straight into the arrest of Jesus and to Peter's denial of him.

Paul's Supper

The impact of the Last Supper was so great that it appears elsewhere in key New Testament writings, not least those of Paul. He, of course, was not one of the Twelve and was not counted among the intimates of Jesus; nevertheless he provides firm references for the meal that had, we assume, become common to the Christians he knew. Once more the betrayal element is present for when he raises the issue of the special Christian meal he writes of it as having its birth in the night 'when he was betrayed' (1 Corinthians 11: 23–26). In this first letter to the Corinthians there is an interesting feature that seems to develop this otherwise brief mention of betrayal. It takes the form of a discussion of what he calls eating the bread or drinking the cup of the Lord 'in an unworthy manner' that makes a person 'guilty of profaning the body and blood of the Lord'. To partake of the bread and wine in such a way is to 'bring judgement upon' oneself. Even more strongly Paul adds a comment that many today would find very hard to accept: that such unworthy participation is the reason why 'many of you are weak and ill, and some have died'.

There are at least two ways we might understand this. The obvious one is to see the religious life as a reflection of our ordinary life that works on the basis of give and take, of work and wages, of simple cause and effect. It is hard to accept this view because one of the absolute key convictions of Paul concerned grace, and grace did not work in that way. Grace is a form of God's generosity, an overflowing of love, mercy and acceptance towards those who lack all hope of earning or meriting anything. Unworthiness could not refer to someone's sin. Certainly Paul is worried about the selfishness in the church at Corinth where people come together for the Lord's Supper but use it as an occasion for their own pleasure, where factions are marked and the rich eat and drink too much in a display of wealth while the poor go hungry (1 Corinthians 11:20–21). Certainly this is not acceptable Christian behaviour because it allows nothing of grace to become evident. But I wonder if there is not another aspect to Paul's chiding of the Corinthians in his reference to them eating and drinking judgement upon themselves. There may well be, because when he chastises the undisciplined Corinthians he begins with that reference to betrayal just mentioned above. Paul believes that the tradition he had passed on to the Corinthians was one he had 'received from the Lord'. What he had passed on to them was that, 'the Lord Jesus on the night when he was betrayed' had taken bread, given thanks and broken it and said that it was his body and that they should do this in remembrance of him (1 Corinthians 11:23–26). To profane the body of Christ symbolized in the bread seems to provide a strong echo of the betrayal of Christ himself at the Last Supper by Judas. While this may or may not be a proper interpretation of Paul the point that is clear is that betrayal was an essential part of the framework of the Supper as Paul believed himself to have received it from Christ. And that reception was, it would seem, something of a religious experience, a vision or insight because, as we have already noted, Paul had never met the earthly Jesus. He did, however, in the strongest of terms, stake his claim to being an apostle on a special revelation of Christ to him both on the road to Damascus, when he was first converted to Christianity, and in subsequent religious experiences. The very mention of betrayal by Paul is all the more significant precisely because he was not part of the first group of disciples. It means that early Christian tradition associated the Lord's Supper with betrayal. Since Paul's letters were probably written before the Gospels we cannot expect him to have gained the idea from any written texts but from the oral tradition, from the teachings and the grapevine existing among the earliest disciples.

Eucharistic Betrayal

At the beginning of this chapter I asked why betrayal plays an insignificant part in contemporary forms of Eucharist and in the beliefs associated with that rite. Part of the answer lies in the difficulty we face in accepting the abandonment and betrayal of Christ (see chapter 8). Another possibility is that betrayal does, actually, play an ongoing part in Christian spirituality but in a deeply implicit way. In the Eucharist, for example, there is a strong sense of confession of sin and its forgiveness. This can easily bring before the mind's eye an awareness of lack of loyalty and commitment to Christ and to the way of the Kingdom of God which he followed and in which we, ourselves, become involved through baptism.

Even so, the very expression, 'in the same night that he was betrayed', is, perhaps, too familiar to those who regularly attend the Eucharist. This expression is, after all, a remarkable way of bringing the mind to a focus in the service of the Lord's Supper. It is a constant reminder of the betrayal underlying Jesus' life-experience. Part of the argument of this book is that, once we appreciate that betrayal is not the single act of the one single man, Judas, but was a feature of the lives of those caught up with Jesus of

Nazareth, these eucharistic words become more all-embracing. It is not that someone else has betrayed him, but that we have betrayed him.

The earliest community of faith was also a community of betrayers. This is a very hard thing to say and contradicts much of our normal view of those earliest Christians. But to announce in the community of faith that it was 'in the same night that he was betrayed that he took the cup' is to say a great deal about the members of that community as well as about today's community of faith. There is great power in these words with two features standing out from them. One of these is passive and one active. In a passive sense Jesus was betrayed: it was something that happened to him. While in the active sense, Jesus took the cup: it was something he did. That cup, in itself, carries a depth of significance for subsequent Christians. For the earliest Christians, who were largely Jewish, it stands for the cup of wine that he took to bless at the Passover meal that changed its focus from the ancient memory of Egyptian captivity to a new community grounded in Jesus and his forthcoming death. For subsequent generations the cup reflected a thanksgiving of those who believed they, too, had been redeemed and had come to salvation through Jesus within the context of a new community. But the very idea of 'the cup' also echoes the words of Jesus that come in the Garden of Gethsemane when he asked that, if possible, 'this cup' be taken from him: a 'cup' that he, nevertheless, accepts.

Betraying Fellowship

To conclude this chapter on the Supper we bring the theme of betrayal from its normal hidden position into sharp focus through one specific ritual drawn from the Maundy

Thursday liturgy of Durham Cathedral. It was practised in the fourteenth century and was revived only in 1998. It has been observed on Maundy Thursday for the last few years since then as the Judas Cup Ceremony.[1] It takes place after the celebration of the Lord's Supper on Maundy Thursday evening using a large cup or bowl called a mazer, but not the Communion chalice. This vessel was once called the Judas Cup because the face of Judas was worked into its bowl so that when the monks drank from it they could see, as it were, the face of Judas looking at them and, in a sense, mirroring their own face. Here I describe the year 2000 event and present it in the form of the service used, to allow it to speak for itself. I also include the brief introduction that was included in this service, composed by one of the current cathedral clergy and expressing in a natural and direct way much of what underlies the theme of betrayal and faith expressed throughout this book.

The Judas Cup Ceremony

Maundy Thursday is the day on which we recall the ambiguities of discipleship even among the most committed of us. Of those privileged to be present at the Last Supper, one disciple was already plotting Jesus' betrayal, while another would soon deny any knowledge of him and subsequently weep tears of penitence. In the medieval monastery at Durham those ambiguities were recalled in a ceremony called the Judas Cup. The dramatic re-enactment below is

1. I am grateful to John McKinnell of Durham's Department of English whose scholarly research drew attention to this ancient Durham rite and to the current Cathedral Chapter for agreeing that I might reproduce their version of this service here.

an attempt to translate that ritual into modern terms as a way of reminding us of the necessity for humility as we recall the ambiguities of our own discipleship.

Choir: Psalm 22:1–11.

The dean leads the clergy to a table set in the Quire.

Dean: As they sat at supper, Jesus said, 'Truly I tell you, one of you will betray me – one who is eating with me'. At this they were distressed, and one by one they said to him, 'Surely you do not mean me?'
'It is one of the Twelve,' he said, 'who is dipping into the bowl with me.'

The Celebrant places the mazer on the table and pours wine into it from an earthenware jug.

Celebrant: Alas for the man by whom the Son of man is betrayed.

Dean: Lord, is it I?

Clergy and
congregation: Lord, is it I?

The Dean then drinks from the mazer and passes it to the other clergy present. Each in turn drinks from it in silence.

Dean: Even if I were to die with you, I will never disown you.

Celebrant: And they all said the same.

Clergy and
congregation: Even if I have to die with you, I will never disown you.

Celebrant: It was night.

The lights in the Quire are dimmed as the table is cleared and the clergy depart. The celebrant returns to the High Altar and proceeds with the Stripping of the Altar.

The Garden Betrayal

Christians have paid relatively little attention to what befell Jesus in the Garden of Gethsemane compared with what happened to him at the Last Supper and on Calvary. This is as true for artists as it is for theologians. There are innumerable paintings of the Crucifixion but relatively few dealing with Christ's Passion in the garden. So, too, with theology: there is much written about the Eucharist and Christ's death but much less on his personal trial in the garden. While this is quite understandable, given the centrality of the death of Christ in Christian theories about salvation and in the Eucharist, it is still slightly surprising in the light of the extent of the Gospel narratives. In this book I am trying to redress the balance, if only a little. In this chapter we see how the garden scene follows on from the Supper and brings to light further facets of the cluster of betrayal. Here Peter, James and John all have their parts to play, as does Judas.

Rudolph Otto, a theologian of the late nineteenth century, is one of the few to draw our attention to Christ's agony in the Garden of Gethsemane. He asks if it was the fear of death that brought Jesus to this state, and he answers 'no'. It was not any simple fear of death or facing up to death that brought on the 'sore amazement', but a sense of heaviness and of a life so much 'shaken to its depths' that he was 'exceeding sorrowful even unto death'. Otto suggests that what we glimpse here is one who, as a human being, encounters the deep mystery of God. This is something difficult for contemporary Christians to accept because we are so used to thinking and talking about Jesus as the divine Son of God that we find it hard to think of him in terms of human nature. But Otto's outlook is very instructive, helping us to gain some understanding of the challenge that Jesus saw facing him, as an individual without any magical or supernatural force protecting him from the stark reality of his situation. Otto also tries to pinpoint the strangeness of what Jesus encountered. The sense of a mystery that has an attraction and yet a repulsion in it is reflected at one and the same time in the sayings, 'take this cup away', and 'thy will not mine be done'.

Betrayal

Earlier we dwelt on the cluster of ideas surrounding betrayal as a foundational aspect of earliest Christianity. Because it is such a strong underlying current of the Passion of Christ and of his disciples it merits a treatment all of its own. In answer to the question of why the Gospels dwell so much on betrayal, it is not sufficient to suggest, as a very simple reading of John's Gospel might encourage, that Judas' betrayal lay in his simple identification of Jesus for the authorities by pointing him out to them. Certainly it is inadequate to argue that Judas simply knew where Jesus was likely to be (John 18:2). Jesus and his disciples would hardly have been difficult to locate if people had wanted to find them. No, betrayal is deeper than that and extends across a variety of the Gospel events. Its central depth lies in discipleship, in the nature of the relationship between master and disciple, and in profound disturbances of that relationship.

In approaching this ruptured realm between Jesus and his disciples we need a clear vision of a strand of theology that is easily overlooked in the Gospels though it is, perhaps, clearer in John than in Matthew, Mark or Luke. This concerns the very closeness of Jesus and his disciples. It focuses on the disciples and their rabbi as a tight-knit group. This picture tends to be far removed from our normal attitude towards the disciples, largely because Jesus has been made to stand out from them as the one, strong, focal point of Christian belief. Because the theology of the Creeds, the practice of the Early Church and today's patterns of worship mark him as divine, our reading of the New Testament often draws a distinction that separates Jesus from all those around him. He walks as a lone actor amid a crowd of supporters. There are biblical texts that encourage this position, and there is much in Christian life and worship that reinforces it. But it is possible, and in the context of this book highly desirable, that we approach these same documents and experiences in another frame of mind to link Jesus with those around him. That is the way I suggest we approach the passions described in this book.

Jesus is a teacher who calls disciples, and sets out to live with them and to show them something of the Kingdom of God. That Kingdom has a degree of mystery to it and involves seeing people and events in such a way that life comes to be lived ethically and sincerely before God. There is something of simplicity about this, so much so that Jesus tells the disciples that they need to become rather like children in order to see it at all. It involves a sense of intimacy with God who is just like a father. God knows what we want, knows our inner desires and prayers and prefers the genuineness of those who pray in secret to any public demonstration of piety. This Kingdom is one in which love and mercy replace hatred and authoritarian legalism. Not least, it is open and inclusive rather than closed and exclusive. Those who are in this Kingdom need this perspective because it reflects God's perspective. But, and this introduces a more negative train of thought, to live in this sort of kingdom involves a degree of self-sacrifice. It is a kingdom experienced rather than discussed, acquired through contact more than being learned. Indeed, it was by being with Jesus that the disciples should have gained their insight into it. The story of the Passion of Christ, coming as it does at the close of his ministry, is a story of half-learning. It shows how far, or rather how little, the disciples had entered into Jesus' own vision of the Kingdom of God in their own insight and way of life. This is not surprising since we can presume that this was something Jesus was working out in his own life. Even with the wisdom of hindsight and with 2000 years of Christian history it is still far from easy to be precise about what 'the Kingdom of God' really means. The idea of the Kingdom of God had already been much debated before the time of Jesus, as it was in his day and has been since. It is too much to ask that a group of disciples should arrive at a clear and focused grasp of a crisp idea as though it was a formula to be learned. Ideas of God ruling his people through prophets and priests, through a system of divine laws, or even through kings all played their part. The idea of a Messiah, God's specially anointed one, also had a role in sketching a picture of what a divine rule would be like. The whole issue was, of course, made more complex when the land believed to have been given to the Jews by God was under foreign control.

Far more than some idea of history or philosophy the Kingdom of God was a passionate task of life and, as we have already indicated, it involved sincerity to God who knew us like a father and sought a sense of love and justice among human beings. That goal was, however, extremely challenging because of the way human nature influenced life at all levels. Jesus was setting himself the task of bringing these truths to light within the culture of his own people and amid their religious traditions. But politics and power could not be escaped. A strong religious culture is, in many ways, the worst context in which to be radically religious. Moments of deep religious understanding and action come to be tamed with time and brought under the control of convention.

But there is another important question that we need to ask ourselves. Can we, in any case, really know just what it was that Jesus saw lying before him? The traditional answer to this is a resounding 'yes', on the basis that he knew that he was the divine Son come as the sacrifice for sin and for the redemption of the world. But this is an inadequate and perhaps even unfaithful way of understanding Christ's life, most especially now as he sets his face to go to Jerusalem, for it tends to underplay his Passion. It is, of course, understandable that some might well wish to avoid the pain and anguish of it, but the Gospel accounts demand more than a superficial gloss. There is a tendency among some when talking of the Passion of Christ always to add to any event the additional scene of the Resurrection. They find it hard to speak of these events without adding on a reference to Easter Day. Throughout this book I have sought to avoid that temptation so that our minds may not be diverted from the Gospel accounts of the suffering of Christ and from the responses of the disciples and others.

The Disciples' Failure

I will emphasize this perspective precisely because, in one sense, the Passion story is a story of failure. The disciple-group had not worked. They had not acquired an insight into the Kingdom, or at least it was so partial that its distortion was worse than ignorance. John's Gospel pinpoints this when the disciples tell Jesus they now know that he is 'speaking plainly'; that they know he comes from God and that he knows everything. In the words of John, Jesus simply replies, 'Do you now believe?' Then follow the words, 'The hour is coming, indeed it has come, when you will be scattered, every man to his home, and you will leave me alone' (John 16:29, 32). In the Passion we see the unravelling of discipleship, in different ways and to varying degrees. It is a time of disruption and testing. But, and this is an important point, it was also a fragmentation that would become transformed. With time and with experience these disciples would join together again and when doing so would find themselves inspired by the very life of Christ. The Christian groups of the Acts of the Apostles are Spirit-inspired groups, and the congregations addressed by Paul are described as parts of the very body of Christ. The Passion prepares them for their future and for Christ's future in the world. But for now, for the moment, all is not triumph.

To understand Jesus involves understanding his disciples, just as to understand the early Christians is to understand their congregational or corporate life. So it is that Jesus of Nazareth is presented very much as the man Jesus plus his disciples. They were important for him; they were, it seems, just like his family, or even more important than his family. Remember that when in Matthew's Gospel he is told that his mother and brothers have come to speak to him he replies, 'Who is my mother and my brothers? And stretching out his hand towards his disciples he said, "Here are my mother and my brothers!"' (Matthew 12:46–50). This is a strong affirmation of his disciples, of the group within which his teaching about the Kingdom of God has opportunity to develop. The story of the Gospels is a story of this group. In Mark's Gospel the very start of Jesus' ministry lies in calling four of these men to follow him, we are not even told that they were baptized. Soon afterwards he selected those who would become the Twelve (Mark 1:16; 3:13–19).

Betrayal only makes sense in the light of this group of disciples, this band within which Jesus sought to make clear the way to live in God's Kingdom. They were given their own opportunity to share in the power that came from that form of Kingdom living (Mark 6:7–13). Yet they did not always see the point; Mark even speaks of their hardened hearts (Mark 6:52; 8:17). At the pivotal point of Mark's Gospel Jesus talks about saving one's life or losing it, and asks what profit there might be in gaining the whole world and losing one's self (Mark 8:36). The whole point is that Jesus needs the disciples with him as he shows what it means to be the Kingdom of God.

To be one of the disciples was to develop particular attitudes that expressed the Kingdom of God. These very attitudes contradicted the negative values that are found within the cluster of betrayal, including being ashamed of Jesus as the one who taught about the Kingdom (Mark 8:38). Obviously denial is one of the negative values (Matthew 10:33), as are thoughts of blasphemy against the truth (Mark 3:29). Blasphemy itself seems to reveal a combination of shame combined with denial – at least these attitudes bear a degree of family resemblance between them. They are values that should be alien among the disciples.

It is no accident that it is at the Passover meal, or in John's Gospel at a meal on the night before, that the issue of betrayal emerges so powerfully. The context of the meal was just that of fellowship and of an intense friendship between Jesus and the disciples. It was also a time when Jesus was extremely troubled within himself. Here there is a strange parallel, for John's Gospel speaks of Jesus as much troubled at this meal while Matthew, for example, pinpoints this deep inner distress as taking place in the Garden of Gethsemane (Matthew 26:38). In John's Gospel Jesus does go with his disciples into a garden, the place where he is arrested, and where Judas betrays him with the kiss, and it is there, too, that he accepts 'the cup that the father has given' him: he tells Peter that in clear tones (John 18:11). The agony in the garden in John's Gospel becomes the agony of moving in the direction of God's will and the betrayal in the garden is yet another, though profoundly disturbing, betrayal of that journey and takes several forms.

The least obvious and, at first sight, the least offensive betrayal in the passages we have looked at so far concerns the sleeping disciples. After the Last Supper the disciples go with Jesus into the Garden of Gethsemane. Taking Peter, James and John with him Jesus moves apart and 'begins to be greatly distressed and troubled'. He tells them that his 'soul is very sorrowful, even to death' and asks them to stay and watch. This is an unusual and distinctive part of the Gospel narratives, for Jesus has not been described as being in this kind of condition before. It contrasts very starkly, for example, with Mark's earlier account of the Trans- figuration of Jesus. Then, too, he had taken Peter, James and John with him to a mountain when he became, drama- tically, associated with Elijah and Moses, two of the greatest figures from ancient Jewish tradition (Mark

9:2–8). On that occasion these disciples had responded by wanting to set up three tents as places for these holy persons to inhabit, echoing the idea that in the Old Testament a tent had been pitched as a kind of dwelling-place of God long before a solid temple was built. The way Mark writes his Gospel hints at a potentially similar situation as the disciples entered the garden with Jesus and as he tells them to be watchful and on the alert: perhaps something dramatic may occur yet again. Against that background it is almost unbelievable that they should fall asleep. But fall asleep they do even though they are told that he is extremely sorrowful, so pressed by things that he even feels death pressing upon him.

Jesus turns to pray but on three occasions he returns only to find the disciples asleep. On the first occasion he addresses Peter, using his old name of Simon: 'Simon, could you not remain alert for one hour?' Then he tells him, once more, to watch and to pray lest he, too, enters into temptation. Then come the words that have entered into the English language, 'the spirit is willing but the flesh is weak' (Mark 14:38). And sleep they do in the weakness of their flesh. When he returns the third time to find the sleepers sleeping he tells them to get up because the time of betrayal has come. But what of the sleepers and their sleep? In the flow of this Gospel their behaviour constitutes yet another form of betraying his journey. At the moment when he most needed their presence and support and actually asks for it, it is denied. In a most subtle way Mark shows how much the spotlight falls on Jesus and on Jesus alone. The pattern of his being abandoned begins to take firmer shape.

Final Moments

And what of Christ as he prays alone in Gethsemane? His is a prayer seeking deliverance. First he asks that, if it is possible, 'the hour might pass' from him. Then, addressing God by the familiar term for father, 'Abba' – an unusual practice for his day – he asks that if it is at all possible 'remove this cup from me'. There is a starkness and direct-ness in this prayer that impresses us in its simplicity, all the more so since throughout Mark's Gospel Jesus has predicted suffering and betrayal. Now that the moment comes he asks to be delivered from it. The humanity of this request is part of its saving expression. We can feel with him in what he says. Even though we do not know the depth of his grasp of what was going on we, too, have been in situations that we would prefer to avoid. In our own small and not so small ways we know what it is to ask that an hour might pass from us.

But Jesus does not stop there. For his life, and the journey upon which he set himself in coming to Jerusalem, had the very idea of losing one's life at their heart. So it is that his prayer for deliverance is completed by the wish that God's will and not his own will be done. This makes the prayer all the more painful and realistic. There is no bargaining with God but only the final acknowledgement that God is God. In this garden scene we are presented with three worlds in which Jesus is caught up. Worlds that are worlds apart from each other, and yet worlds that were all too real for Jesus of Nazareth now set amid his destiny at Jerusalem. There is the relationship with his Father, with his disciples and with the arresting party. Three spheres of involvement, three realms of identity: the son, the rabbi and the criminal.

It is now, as the son of his heavenly Father, that his iden-tity as the rabbi leads him into arrest as a criminal, for

Judas approaches with the arresting crowd and greets him with the word 'Rabbi'. This image of Judas betraying Jesus with a kiss needs careful consideration because it is not part of all the Gospel accounts. Mark and Matthew do describe Judas as kissing Jesus and addressing him as 'Rabbi' (Mark 14:45; Matthew 26:49). In Luke the suggestion is that it was just as Judas was about to greet Jesus in this way that Jesus took the initiative and asked him whether he would betray him with a kiss (Luke 22:48). In John's Gospel there is no suggestion of any greeting or kiss between Judas and Jesus: it simply refers to Judas, 'who betrayed him' (John 18:2).

What is deeply significant about the garden event in John's Gospel is not simply the role of Judas in organizing a band of soldiers as an arresting party but the way in which an additional spotlight falls on Peter. It is he who uses a sword to defend Jesus (as presumably he sees it), but in so doing prompts Jesus to ask whether he should not take the cup given to him by the Father. To the eye of faith looking at the Garden of Gethsemane it is not hard to see a shadow of the Garden of Eden. In symbolic terms the first Adam had disobeyed the voice of the Lord his God and was driven from that garden paradise. Here in the language of Paul the apostle, the second Adam obeys the divine call and is taken from the garden.

Paul's Passion

As mentioned in previous chapters, it has become traditional to use only the Gospels when describing and reflecting upon the Passion of Christ. The obvious reason for this is that the major accounts of Jesus and his suffering lie largely in the Gospel accounts of his life. Our focus has, however, widened from that conventional approach to Christ's Passion to include other individuals and their passions, all in relation to those acts and motives that constitute what I have called the cluster of betrayal.

Now we take yet a further step to include Paul and what might be called Paul's passion, and to see how his acts and motives share in the experience of the earliest Christians. Some might find this an unusual step to take since he does not appear in the Gospel stories and was not one of the original disciples of Christ, nor was he involved in the events surrounding Christ's Passion. But – and this is an important issue as far as this book is concerned – the New Testament was written through faith and for faith. It comes from early believers committed to a belief that Jesus of Nazareth had been specially related to God as the one who brought salvation to them. Its various Gospels and even some letters, such as the letter to the Hebrews, all give an account of the life of Jesus in such a way as to make him central to understanding God and the ways God dealt with men and women. Throughout those documents it spells out the implications of belief and sketches how people should live. All in all the New Testament shows us that there were strong groups of Christians from whom all this written material came. It shows that there were communities of faith concerned to express a strong sense of change that people experienced in and through a new sense of identity as Christians. The very name 'Christian' was new just as the communities it described were new.

Betrayal and Denial

One individual who was of fundamental importance for some of these new communities was Paul, also known as Saul of Tarsus. We turn our attention to him because of his influential status as an early Christian leader and, in particular, as one who also experienced something of a passion of his own, one that was intimately related to the Passion of Christ. By doing this we add another example of the way in which the Passion of Christ touches the depths of the lives of others and we also come to see how profoundly the very idea of Christ's Passion continued to influence the developing Christian churches of the Mediterranean world.

We are now familiar with the importance of denial and betrayal in the Gospels and have come to see that, perhaps, denial was a more significant part of earliest Christian life than our current understanding of the New Testament often appreciates. We have already noted that Paul's epistles were, in all probability, written earlier than the Gospels, a fact that must always be highlighted especially since the Gospels are placed in front of them in our New Testament. For a few readers there is an almost unconscious sense that what comes first in the book must have been first in time, and that is almost certainly not the case. It is possible, and perhaps probable, that Paul did not know any of the Gospels. What he did know was what the earliest Christians said about Jesus and his teaching. He also knew his own experience, and what he reckoned to be his own encounter with the resurrected Jesus. And this is a crucial point, for if Paul did not know the Gospels as formal documents and yet reflects the theme of betrayal then it is very likely that he does so precisely because it was a wide-spread attitude established among the earliest believing communities.

In Paul's second letter to Timothy (2:11–13) there is a text that refers to a 'true saying', to some widely shared idea expressed in a phrase, poem or even a song. It is presented as a kind of poem and stands out from the surrounding chapter and touches on this very issue of betrayal.

> For if we have died with him we shall also live with him.
> If we have endured with him we shall also rule with him.
> If we deny him he will deny us.
> If we are faithless, he remains faithful
> For he is not able to deny himself.

Here denial is a repeating motif in what sounds rather like a popular or common saying among Christians. There would, in fact, be no point in using it in the letter if it did not already have some currency among the readers, much as today a preacher may use familiar words from a hymn or from the liturgy to emphasize a broader point. While it is unwise to speculate too freely on this issue it is, at least, worth pondering whether other New Testament verses on betrayal and denial also echo a cultural motif of early Christianity. If, for example, the text in the first letter of John saying that 'no one who denies the Son has the Father' (1 John 2:23) did possess such a familiar background its significance would be greater than the simple meaning of the words would otherwise indicate. They would be words

rooted in emotional power. Similarly, denial is seen as
something that Peter raises in accusation against the Jews
at the temple in his speech in Acts when he tells them that
they had delivered up and denied Jesus (Acts 3:13, 14).
Here the idea of delivering up or handing over echoes what
would emerge in the Gospel accounts of the garden arrest.

Paul's Betrayal

But what of Paul? My prime concern here is to suggest that
Paul is so well aware of this Christian motif of denial that
he describes his own life and religious experience in terms
of it. This becomes apparent when Paul describes himself
as the last of the apostles, and as one unfit to be called
an apostle 'because I persecuted the church of God (1
Corinthians 15:9). The fuller story of his persecution of the
Church is given in the Acts of the Apostles where, as Saul
(before the time when he is more regularly called Paul), he
was present at the stoning to death of Stephen, the first
Christian martyr. In Stephen's last speech, which triggered
the wrath of the authorities and brought death upon him,
he describes them as having 'betrayed and murdered' the
Righteous One (Acts 7:52). As he is stoned the crowd is
said to have left their clothes at Saul's feet while they
stoned Stephen, 'and Saul was consenting to his death'
(Acts 8:1). Shortly afterwards, while actively intent upon
capturing Christians and bringing them to trial Paul is
overtaken by that famous conversion on the road to
Damascus. For our purposes its crucial element lies in
Paul's awareness of the message he believes had come to
him from the resurrected Christ himself who says to him, 'I
am Jesus whom you are persecuting' (Acts 9:5; see also
Acts 26:12–15). This was something deeply fixed in his
memory for, years later, when he was making a defence of

his life before the civil authorities, he recalls that day and
the way the voice from heaven addressed him 'in the
Hebrew language, "Saul, Saul, why do you persecute me"'
(Acts 26:14). And, as Paul tells us, he was not disobedient
to the heavenly vision. Subsequently his life becomes one
of considerable hardship as he seeks to testify to the new
reality of Christ as one who suffers, dies and is raised and
who becomes, as he puts it, one who brings light to the
nations. As far as the writer of the Acts of the Apostles is
concerned there is a strong link forged between Christ and
the ongoing community of Christians into which Paul is
admitted, which he then serves and seeks to expand. But,
when he was still an outsider, his persecution of the group
was a persecution of Christ.

Persecution in Betrayal Cluster

At this point I want to suggest a connection between that
persecution and the denial of Christ described in the
Gospels. There is a sense in which Paul's persecution of
Christians was a persecution of Christ and, deeply embed-
ded in that, lay a denial of Christ and, perhaps, even a
betrayal of Christ. But this last issue is complex, for while
there is a difference between denial and betrayal they are
not totally unrelated. They are part of the betrayal cluster
of ideas. One relatively simple distinction might be that,
for us, denial involves facts or events while betrayal
involves people. We can deny something but we betray
someone.

In Paul's case persecution becomes a form of betrayal
and he can be seen as implying that he, too, has denied
Christ, at least while he was still in his zealous Jewish sense
of identity. In fact, his conversion served the powerful
purpose of bringing him from denial not only to accept-

ance but also to the active furthering of Christ's message (Acts 20:21). The very idea of testimony is the opposite of denial and achieves a high profile in Paul's opening verses of the Epistle to the Romans. There he affirms that he is 'not ashamed of the gospel' for he believes it to be the very power of God for salvation in believers (Romans 1:16).

In the closing chapters of the Acts of the Apostles there emerges an account of what could well be called Paul's Passion. It is hauntingly strange in the way it mirrors, to a degree, the Passion of Christ. Here we need to be particularly careful in the way we express this because while I do not want to forge too strong a link between Christ and Paul neither do I want us to overlook its potential significance. And that is that Paul sets himself the task of going to Jerusalem (Acts 20:16) as one 'bound in the Spirit, not knowing what shall befall me there; except that the Holy Spirit testifies to me in every city that imprisonment and afflictions await me' (Acts 20:22). He even speaks of people who will arise within the Christian fellowship only to destroy it (Acts 20:29). His going to Jerusalem echoes Christ's journey, with the destroyers of the community not being far removed from those who betray Jesus. While it is perfectly possible that these descriptions of Paul's situation and life are simply accidentally reminiscent of aspects of what happened to Jesus they should not be simply ignored without some consideration. The one great difference comes in the fact that Jerusalem was Jesus' destination while, ultimately, Rome turns out to be the final goal of Paul. The one marks the Jewish focus of a culture and the other the centre of the Gentile world.

In Paul's teaching there is a strong awareness that suffering, in the sense of enduring hardship and pain, is a realistic and perhaps even necessary part of his own calling. Indeed, the first Christian who came to him after his dramatic sense of encounter with Christ, Ananias of Damascus, was charged to tell Paul 'how much he would suffer for the sake of my name' (Acts 9:16). This turns out to be the case. There are passages in which Paul rehearses all the suffering he has endured as an apostle with 'countless beatings and often near death'; indeed he gives a catalogue of disasters and distress towards the end of his second letter to the Corinthians (2 Corinthians 11:23–30). His teaching of the way in which all Christians are bound up together as parts of one body involves the sense that when one suffers all suffer (1 Corinthians 12:26). This commitment also becomes the basis for that suffering expressed in Paul's sense of 'daily pressure upon me of my anxiety for all the churches' (2 Corinthians 11:28).

Then there are the occasional insights into his life as when, years after the event, he recalls the heavenly voice at his conversion telling him that 'it hurts you to kick against the goads' (Acts 26:14). There is something very interesting and powerful in those words, words that are not there in the earlier accounts of what happened on the road to Damascus (Acts 9:4–7; 21:6–10). Paul had known some kind of personal hurt involved in his own persecution of the Christians. This reminds us of our earlier considerations of the way in which the betrayal of another involves a degree of betrayal of ourselves. So, too, with Paul. At a less psychological level there was also that 'thorn in the flesh', some illness or besetting problem whose identity we do not actually know, but which led Paul to 'beseech the Lord about this, that it should leave me'. This he did three times but the divine response was that 'my grace is sufficient for you, for my power is made perfect in weakness' (2 Corinthians 12: 7–8).

Apostleship and Betrayal

The outcome of these reflections is to suggest that Paul understood very well that betrayal was a powerful theme of the earliest Christians. More than that, his own sense of identity as an apostle gained a degree of authenticity through the very fact that, in his own way, he too had denied Christ. But, just as the other disciples who had fled and abandoned Christ had regrouped and gained an entirely new sense of purpose through the resurrection experience, so with himself. He also possessed a resurrection experience and, through it, had come to an understanding of grace. This very idea of grace, the sense of God's purposeful love experienced as a generous and unwarranted goodwill, had overwhelmed Paul. Grace was now the atmosphere he breathed. It was the message of divine forgiveness and took shape among a community of people viewing themselves as brothers and sisters. What is more, they knew the power and significance of grace all the more greatly because of their betrayal.

There is a dramatic gap between the disciples who fled and left Christ to his death and the disciples who regrouped and gained a profound sense that they had not been abandoned or, should we even say it, that they had not been betrayed. This may be the sense of that text in John's Gospel, itself very likely a late writing, that expressed the spirituality of at least one of the early Christian groups, describing Jesus as saying to his disciples that he would not leave them desolate, as orphans (John 14:18). Whatever they had done to him he would not do to them.

Above all, they existed as a group. Paul uses the image of the body of Christ made up of each individual Christian with a duty to perform in the world at large. What is clear in Paul is that there is a passion underlying Christian conviction, not simply for him as an apostle, but for all. To be a Christian inevitably involves a sharing of pain, or a bearing of one another's burdens. Passion underlies the Christian way of life.

In concluding our thoughts on Paul's passion we should, perhaps, not allow the negative emotions to fill the picture completely. Because Christianity does pay considerable attention to pain, suffering and death it is easy for some individuals to take this to excess and, almost, to enjoy this dimension of life. There is no virtue in pain and sadness and it always needs to be set in the wider framework of grace and of the care that people give each other. It is sometimes possible for individuals almost to enjoy their suffering and not to want to break through it into a sense of joy or fulfilment. It is here that Christianity speaks in a balanced way, acknowledging that sickness is balanced by health as sorrow is by joy. The fact that there are periods of the Christian year, just as there are periods in our individual lives, when the dimension of suffering takes centre stage is of importance, but the issue of balance always needs to be at the back of one's mind. Indeed, in talking of balance it may well be that this aspect of passion is well worth emphasizing at the present time, given a tendency for some Christian groups to highlight joy, health and the flourishing aspects of faith and to give the impression that someone whose life is hard, and whose way is difficult has, somehow, wandered from the true path of discipleship. Certainly, as far as the New Testament is concerned, the Christian life is neither pure bliss nor pure torture, and that weighting needs ever to be recalled. Lest that might ever be forgotten we now turn to Christ's Passion, the heart of the faith of many rooted in a place where a heart was broken.

8

The Death of Christ

'Jesus Christ suffered under Pontius Pilate, was crucified, dead and buried'. This statement, from one of the great Christian Creeds, is regularly recited by millions of believers the world over. It summarizes part of the core of Christianity and sets Christ's Passion firmly before the eye of faith. We have followed Jesus on his personal pilgrimage to Jerusalem, his journey into death through betrayal. It is now time to watch with him as the events of his last few days of earthly life unfold and as forces from the cluster of betrayal come to make their presence felt.

Mocking

Misunderstood by many of his disciples, betrayed by Judas, arrested and 'processed' by the religious and secular authorities, including Pilate, Jesus comes to be mocked by the soldiers. Here, at least, there is little explicit betrayal or denial. These are no friends or disciples but men with a job to do: unpleasant men, perhaps, but certainly with an unpleasant job. They mock him as they had probably mocked many others. Their accusation of him being King of the Jews prompt them to mock him by draping him in a mock regal cloak and a crown of thorns.

As the Gospel writers tell their story, events seem to have been turned on their head. Jesus the miracle worker, the man who attracted disciples and announced God's Kingdom has come to nothing. Any success as Messiah has gone. This man from the regions has fallen under the political authority of Rome, just as he has been rejected by the religious authorities of his own people. This mocking with a false robe, a false crown (and in Matthew's Gospel also with a reed to represent a false rod of office), all makes great sense. People may claim power and authority but, in the end, they fail. So the acclamation, 'Hail King of the Jews', becomes the cynical jesting of those who kneel in false homage (Mark 15:19). All this marks failure. But this is precisely where Christians look back and read the events with the wisdom of hindsight and the eye of faith. Yes, affirm the generations of ages, he was a king, he did command homage, but his power was not that of an earthly monarch. In the deepest of senses these soldiers did not know what they were doing. In their callousness they spoke a higher truth; their false words would become invested with honour by countless future believers. Their bending of the knee in homage would lead descendants in the faith to speak of him as the one at whose name every knee should bow in genuine devotion. But for now, in that situation, and devoid of the retrospective eye, Jesus stands silent as his Passion deepens. So they take off the soldier's coloured cloak and put his own clothes back on him and lead him out to crucify him.

And then, for a moment, for a brief but telling moment, the same soldiers compel a passerby to carry his cross for him. This man, Simon of Cyrene, is identified as the father of Alexander and Rufus, names that are used by Mark in a familiar way, as though readers would know who they were, seemingly implying that they were Christian. Of Simon we know only that he helped carry Jesus' cross. This might have been unusual in that it appears to have been normal for condemned men to carry their own cross which suggests that Jesus was, at this point, too weak to do so.

Crucifixion

He is crucified. This is so simply stated by the Gospels that they do not linger over this part of Christ's Passion. He refuses the drugged wine, thereby accepting the final pain and anguish of his situation. The symbolic 'cup' that, in Gethsemane, he had asked to have taken from him if at all possible, he now accepts in his suffering. By not accepting the actual 'cup' with its pain-relieving liquor he fully accepts the symbolic 'cup' and his Passion draws towards its climax.

His clothes are taken from him and like others he would have been crucified naked. Here that process of denial and betrayal that began as he set out on the road to Jerusalem reaches its peak. His friends and disciples have gone; his clothes are taken. What is left for him? Certainly he has a title, the ironic and mocking title, placed on his cross: 'The King of the Jews' (Mark 15:26).

But he also has two criminal companions crucified alongside him, and there are the inevitable members of the crowd. These add insult to injury, goading him with their observations that he cannot save himself even though he said he could rebuild the temple in three days. So too with the chief priests who touch that other aspect of healing and miracles in Jesus' ministry: 'He saved others but he cannot save himself'. Certainly, Jesus has come to nothing and everyone who is still around reminds him of that fact. Neither as Messiah nor as a miracle worker has his life come to fruition. So it was that Jesus of Nazareth was crucified at about nine o'clock in the morning. Three hours later darkness fell over the land and after another three hours Jesus died – some six hours of final suffering.

Final Betrayal?

Mark's and Matthew's Gospels give a very similar account of these last hours. They draw particular attention to what Jesus said, and what they record is nothing more and nothing less than the question. 'My God, my God, why hast thou forsaken me?' (Matthew 27:45; Mark 15:34). These Gospels also record that when he died he uttered a loud cry, but they give us no actual words. Luke's Gospel, however, does provide words for that final cry, as Jesus says, 'Father, into thy hands I commend my spirit' (Luke 23:46). As we have already observed, the Gospels of Matthew, Mark and Luke are often called the Synoptic Gospels precisely because they regularly adopt a similar outlook and summary on the life of Jesus. But there are occasions when they do diverge from each other in telling ways, and this is the case with the words from the cross.

Even so, as a group, they often differ significantly from John's Gospel which has a distinctive theological purpose all of its own, something that becomes very apparent with the Crucifixion. John sets the Crucifixion at noon, at the time the Passover lambs would be killed for the Jewish festival of Passover. John also gives quite different words of Jesus from the cross than do the Synoptic Gospels. In John, Jesus talks to his mother and to his 'beloved disciple' and links them in a mutual bond of care. He then says, 'I thirst' and, finally, 'It is finished' (John 19:26–30). For John the Crucifixion is, fundamentally, a sacrifice. Even though he gives us more words from the cross than do the other Gospels it is less the words themselves than what is done to Jesus and what is achieved through him that counts. By having Jesus crucified at the time of the killing of the Passover lambs John makes the powerful point that Jesus is the true Passover Lamb given to save his people from death and to deliver them from bondage.

Then a soldier pierces his side and out flow blood and water, which Christian tradition has long interpreted as referring to the Eucharist (John 19:34). In fact the Crucifixion itself is not described in Matthew, Mark and Luke in terms of any blood at all, nor is it in John's Gospel up until this moment when Jesus is speared. This is an interesting point, especially bearing in mind the accounts of the Last Supper and the link made there between Jesus' blood and the forgiveness of sins. Perhaps these synoptic authors thought that they had so presented the Last Supper that the Crucifixion could simply be left to speak for itself. Certainly, many Christian traditions have stressed the blood of sacrifice in connection with the Crucifixion as they have developed the theme of salvation and interpreted the one in terms of the other. Throughout the New Testament there are very many references to the blood of Christ as blood of atonement that brings God and humanity together through forgiveness and redemption. Indeed, such references are so extensive that there is little point even in singling out particular examples. Rather, let us focus on what Matthew, Mark and Luke do say, and say with considerable power about Jesus at his final moment.

Forsaken

Matthew, Mark and Luke all bring our attention to the central words from the cross and confront us with the terrible question of abandonment. 'My God, my God, why hast thou forsaken me?' Throughout the centuries believers have found great difficulty with these words and have tried to interpret them in ways that confer upon them a positive meaning in place of their apparent stark awfulness. One commentator, for example, suggests that Luke adds the additional words 'Father, into thy hands I commend my spirit' in order to 'suppress the anxious-making thought that the Lord might have lost his faith' (Goulder 1989: 769). These are, indeed, difficult issues precisely because we are hardly in a position to think ourselves into the feelings and beliefs of Jesus. It might even be unwise to project our own ideas of faith and unbelief onto him as though Jesus was a Christian as are members of contemporary Christian Churches. Even these Gospels present a variety of views.

Another favourite explanation is to take Psalm 22 which begins, 'My God, my God why hast thou forsaken me' and to say that Jesus actually had the whole of this psalm in his mind but only uttered its first line. The advantage of that interpretation is that the psalm develops a positive confidence in God as in verse 31, 'But he has saved my life for himself, and my posterity shall serve him', which leaves us with a more satisfying picture of Christ's death. But in the light of what we have explored in earlier chapters of this book on the cluster of denial and betrayal, such interpretations seem misplaced. We cannot tell and certainly do not know what was in Jesus' mind, just as we do not know 'what pain he had to bear', as the great hymn 'There is a Green Hill Far away' puts it. We must remain with what the Gospel writers pass on to us, from faith for faith, and in the case of Mark, as of Matthew, the words are left unadorned and speak of being forsaken. In terms of the pattern of passion we have been tracing through the Gospels it becomes clear that this last moment takes its place in a series of events in which Jesus comes, increasingly, to be left to himself. The rich young ruler decides not to accompany him on his journey to Jerusalem. Peter fails to accept the need for suffering. The disciples sleep while Jesus wrestles with his destiny before his heavenly Father. Judas betrays with a kiss. Jesus is arrested, tried and condemned by the authorities and is rejected by the crowd. In all of this we witness a growing scale of isolation. In each we see a growing tension between Jesus and those involved with him as he pursues his goal. Each shows a degree of commitment to Christ's journey and yet also a degree of withdrawal from it. This tension produces its own degree of passion for each of them, passions that are caught up with each other. Yet, at the end, he stands alone.

It is precisely at this point that a believer, on hearing this Gospel story, expects God to do something. Surely the Almighty, the one Jesus so directly, sincerely and intimately calls Father, will give some sign of help? But nothing happens. There is no saving moment for Jesus. The final terror of abandonment comes.

The Gospel writers see this so clearly. They tell it so directly. Some of the bystanders hear Jesus' cry of dereliction and interpret it as a shout to Elijah, that hero of the Hebrew scriptures who appeared to have been a name used by Jews in times of need. But no help came and Jesus dies. His Passion is concluded. He has lived a life in which he called disciples to share with him in bringing about God's Kingdom. So much had been hopeful and now it had come to this, to a moment of complete human isolation and despair. The common lot of humanity, all at its most negative, now surrounds him. The Kingdom has not come.

Silent Awareness

One of the challenges of this Passion of Christ is a call to dwell on it, to remain with it, and not to flee immediately into what will happen next. For there is a tragedy in this death that must not be overlooked. Christians have regularly glossed over it in many clever ways, noting the sadness but only to offset it by joyous ideas of the forthcoming Resurrection. This rush from Good Friday to Easter Sunday may be a psychological necessity when we feel we cannot bear the strain, but it takes us away from the cross too early and, perhaps, before its depths have taken their effect upon us.

It is not easy to do this because of a powerful tendency in contemporary life to explain everything, and to do so rapidly. The media take the lead in filling in the gaps that life's tragedy, accidents and wickedness produce. People come to feel the need to 'say something' and feel uneasy or inadequate if they have nothing to say. This can often be the case at times of death and bereavement when friends, neighbours and others feel they ought to 'say something', even though they may not know what to say.

In practice, not much needs to be said. Many who are bereaved are quite simply grateful for any kind word or action. They know that, often, there is little that can be said to explain events. The simple fact of shared sympathy in our common lot is adequate enough. More publicly, it is the media that clamour for explanation. No sooner does some tragedy strike than they seek out some authority to comfort the public with a statement about what needs to be done so that such a thing 'may never happen again'. It is as though the fact that life is full of risk has been forgotten. It is as though human beings actually have it in their power to prevent all accidents and catastrophes. It is all an attempt to be safe, and it is sadly futile. The very phrase, 'so that this will never happen again', sounds like a motto of a fearful public longing for safety and security and pinning their hopes on 'the authorities' who should protect them from all hazards.

It is worth asking how that media demand would sound in the case of Jesus. We can imagine the bright young news-reporter asking what should be done so that this tragedy of

Jesus should never happen again. As we ponder the question it becomes absurd. It is like the odd practice of saying a word over and over again until it sounds a stupidly impossible set of sounds. There is a sense in which all the private passions we have considered would have to be different so that this would never happen again. The rich young ruler would have to sell all gladly and follow on the road with Jesus. Peter would have to have that perfect insight into the way of suffering that leads to a losing of life in order to find it. Peter, James and John would learn how to be attentive to the trials of their friend and master. Judas – what of Judas? And what of Pilate and of all others caught up in the life of Christ? And what of ourselves?

In all of this there is a need for silence and for our personal pondering. While theology may, and probably must, produce its own theories of the death of Christ, there is also a very proper human response of silence and wonder. This is one reason why Good Friday services can be of great power when they allow real silence to mix with prayer, hymns and readings, allowing worship to flow through those present as it echoes the depths of our own lives. There is much to learn in the modern life of faith in just being quiet. Children are sometimes told to 'be quiet' when their incessant chatter and questions tire us. So, too, with the children of God. They chatter far too much and far too often, not least in the face of the greatest mysteries and challenges that face us. There is great wisdom in knowing when to be, as it were, spiritually incompetent. Clergy and leaders of worship could benefit greatly from allowing the silence of God's people to overwhelm many a time of otherwise repetitive intercession. Waiting before the cross on Good Friday is one such moment when we cannot control with words the silence of Jesus of Nazareth, let alone of God.

There is also a personal reason for doing so, a kind of practice for our own lives, for the times when we do not understand what is happening to us and no answers are forthcoming. There are many believers who come to their own such moment when they feel forsaken by God and life lies beyond their solid grasp. These are moments when the silent waiting has its place.

Part of the problem of facing these stark words from the cross is that it looks as though God has abandoned Jesus, and this cuts across the expectation of most Christians. It is almost beyond comprehension that God should leave Jesus to whatever might befall him. One traditional form of interpretation argues that because Jesus was a sacrifice for the sins of the world there came a moment when the righteous God could no longer look upon him as he became the focus for all the evil of humankind. God, as it were, turns away his face from the evil and Jesus is abandoned. That view can also leave us with some explicit grasp of Christ's abandonment because we feel there is something we can say to explain it. Such an explanation is most obvious in John's Gospel and something important must be said about this because John differs from Matthew, Mark and Luke in a most significant way and also poses problems for my own argument about the betrayal of Jesus.

John's Supportive Community

Many scholars of the New Testament see the early writings of the first Christians as coming from groups of believers who emphasized different aspects of the life and teaching of Jesus. This is, perhaps, never so clear as in his death and, more particularly, in that betrayal we have highlighted in the Synoptic Gospels. In Matthew, Mark and Luke Jesus is betrayed in many ways, by many people, but in John he is not entirely abandoned. Certainly, Judas does play a large part in John's Gospel and, if anything, he becomes a much more significant agent of evil. Peter, too, denies Christ in a definite fashion. But there remains a small group that stays with Jesus. There is the one described as the beloved disciple, often popularly identified as John. The way this fourth Gospel is written paints a picture of a close intimacy between Jesus as Lord and his followers. They are bound together in a deep spiritual union, almost in a mystical bond of love that is focused in the 'beloved disciple'. In the Last Supper it is to this disciple that Jesus points out Judas as the betrayer (John 13:23). For John's Gospel, Jesus is very much the one in control of all that happens in connection with his death. Even when he speaks of the disciples leaving him, abandoning him or being scattered, it is something that happens to them and not something they do of their own accord. More than that, he tells them that even though they may leave him alone, he will not ultimately be alone because the Father is with him (John 16:32). The odd emphasis in John's Gospel is that God will neither abandon him nor will he and the divine Spirit ever abandon the disciples. The whole of chapters 14 to 17 are about the spiritual power that binds them all together in a community of love and keeps them safe. This reversal of themes is clear in the words 'I will not leave you desolate', where the stress is more on the possibility of the disciples being ultimately abandoned than on Jesus being abandoned (John 14:18). But to return to that disciple whom Jesus loved. When Jesus is arrested this disciple not only follows after him, as does Peter, but he also goes into the high priest's property; indeed it adds that he was 'known to the high priest' (John 18:15). He even gets the servant girl to go and fetch Peter and bring him in.

After Jesus is condemned, and after Peter has denied

Jesus and temporarily disappears from events, the beloved disciple remains and is found standing near to the cross, along with Mary, Jesus' mother (John 19:26). As one commentator puts it, 'there is no abandonment in John, the beloved disciple and Mary are there' (Quast 1989: 89). Jesus addresses them and commits them to each other as adopted mother and son. He says, 'I thirst', and then, 'It is finished'. Here there is no cry of anguish and no sense that God has abandoned him. Then two other figures, Joseph of Arimathea and Nicodemus, one a fearful secret disciple and the other who had come to Jesus by night at the very start of John's Gospel, take the body of Christ and bury it. The message here is that secret disciples become visible. It is as though John's Gospel acknowledges the fact of betrayal as a major feature of the majority of the disciples but not of all. It is almost as though John's Gospel comes from another group of early Christians than those of the tradition represented in Matthew, Mark and Luke. Here I can only hint at this point because our main attention is focused on the other Gospels, and for them the death of Jesus is, very largely, not surrounded by extensive interpretations; it stands as a very challenging and almost unimaginable event. And this is, perhaps, important for today's believers and there may be some benefit in not rushing in with ready answers.

In chapter 6 we thought about the importance of the disciples as the group in which Jesus taught and lived. As Christ's Passion intensified this group ruptured until he was finally left alone. This was a most dramatic feature in the life of Christ and ought not to be forgotten. It is something of profound importance to the Christian Church and to the lives of millions of contemporary individuals for whom loneliness is an aspect of life and of the private passions of life. Jesus taught with great clarity that those who followed with him on the way of God's Kingdom were his mother, sisters and brothers (Mark 3:31–35). Despite denial and fragmentation it would be this strong bond of togetherness that led on to the formation of Christian congregations grounded in the experience of grace and its overspill in mutual concern the one for the other. Just as families are said to hold together because 'blood is thicker than water', so the emerging Christian groups felt a bond of unity of almost unnatural proportion. And the Passion of Jesus lies at its heart. Whenever they meet to eat and drink in remembrance of him they recall that it was 'in the same night that he was betrayed that he took the cup'. If the earliest Christians did, in fact, use this phrase or something like it when they met together for the Lord's Supper it must have struck a deep cord among those few who did share in that cluster of betrayal and in others who knew of it. So it is that, with time, congregations developed their creeds, brief statements to summarize their faith. They included in them the fact that their Master suffered under Pontius Pilate, for the Passion of Jesus lay at the heart of their salvation, of their own lives and their private passions.

9

Death's Passion

From the Passion of Jesus to the passion of our private lives is but a short step, for there is nothing closer to the heart of most lives than experiences of suffering, rejection and hurt. The cluster of acts and motives underlying Christ's Passion is not completely detached from our own existence. Even if we do not often voice them, the destructive effects of evil do influence our personal history and the way we understand ourselves. Our private passions involve things done to us as well as our own self-motivated actions. Both can cause us difficulty. Here, of course, we speak once more of passion in a special way and not simply of the passion of emotional and sexual kinds. By passion, then, we mean the suffering experienced at the hands of others or the distress occasioned by the events and circumstances of life. Such passion involves conflicts over commitments to families, occupation, leisure activities and wider community affairs. They express hopes, ambition, fears and anxieties, and with age and increasing maturity these passions gain in depth and significance. The life of faith also fosters passion as the highest ideals are thwarted in lives that seek the best but sometimes practise the worst. Not least important is the fact of mortality brought before us by the inevitability of events in the death of those we know and of those we love.

Dust thou Art

Within the Christian faith death is a prime concern with the Passion of Christ at its centre. Even so, it is quite easy for people to be active members of congregations for a very long time and hardly ever hear the subject of death being dealt with in any direct way. This is a great shame, but one significant opportunity is presented to us in the profound liturgical theme of Ash Wednesday when we do face our own mortality. In some churches ashes made from the burnt palm leaves used in the Palm Sunday liturgy are placed on the foreheads of the faithful, reminding them of their true status: 'Remember O Man, dust thou art and unto dust thou shalt return'. These are sober and true words that we need to carry close to our heart as we live each day for the realism which should be a hallmark of the Christian.

One of the biggest issues we have to face in our life is death. This is especially important in the present day when death has become a marginal element of life. There are those who want to turn funeral ceremonies into celebrations of life, looking back on the achievements and contributions of the deceased person with family members reading personal poems or scriptures and with music special to the dead person. There is much benefit in this and it takes us forward from the days when the dead were treated almost in an impersonal way at their funeral. But such life-centred funeral celebrations should not obliterate the fact and pain of death. We should not seek to tame death and to domesticate it by taking control of it, for there is no controlling death. This is one fact that Jesus' own response makes very clear.

But – and this is a question that all Christians need to consider for themselves – why should death be a problem for me and for you? One answer is to say that it should not be a problem because Jesus conquered death for everyone and, therefore, nobody need fear death from now on. This is not an easy question to approach for many reasons, including our own individual circumstances but here the example of Jesus' Passion comes to our aid.

Personal Circumstances

One of the greatest facts of life is that nobody really understands another person. Indeed, it is sometimes almost impossible to understand ourselves. This makes the experience of death, including bereavement, very individual but also shows the need for support and the active presence of others. Jesus did not ask his disciples to understand what he was suffering in Gethsemane. He simply told them that the pressure upon him was very great and that they should watch with him. He wanted them near at hand as he endured his own, private, hell. There is something about human suffering that does give people a sympathy towards others, and that is a kind of understanding of great power. When someone tells us that they know what we are going through we can easily tell if they are genuine, even if their own experience was of a different kind. To have them simply support us is a comfort in its own right.

Still, personal circumstances must be given a serious place because each one of us has very different experiences of life and also of death. In terms of bereavement some of us will have experienced the death of those we love and for others that experience still lies ahead. For some bereavement seems a natural end of someone's life while for others it comes as a tragic cutting-off of a life in its prime. For the great majority of people this difference between having experienced grief and not having experienced it is very

great. And even for those who have there can be tremendous differences. Mothers who have lost a baby, a small
child, a teenage son or daughter, or one of their young
married children could tell very different stories. The
fathers, too, would have their own forms of grief that
might be hard to put into words. Older sisters, perhaps
those already grown up and with families of their own, can
often feel a terrible loss when their own adult brother or
sister dies. And then there are partners, husbands and
wives, people who have spent their whole life together and
whose personalities have become intertwined: when one of
them dies it is as though the survivor has also died, at least
in part. And what of children losing one or more of their
parents before they have grown up? And adults, too, losing
their parents in due course? There are those who are struck
by the news of sudden death by accident, those who bear
the suicide of a close relative and those who give years of
their life to supporting someone who is chronically ill
before they die. All have their experiences that mark their
life in some way.

These experiences feed private passions of their own in
many different ways. It is foolish to try to describe them all,
just as research shows that it is extremely unwise to think
too much of fixed stages of grief through which people pass
(Corr 1993). The life history people bring to a bereavement
moulds and forms how they respond and change. For some
a death may even be convenient and bring to an end a
painful and negative relationship; for others it may seem
like the end of the world. Yet there is something about grief
that gives a shared knowledge to those who have known it.
This stems from the sympathy grounded in our common
humanity and from our need for encouragement and the
help of others. There is also, for many, a growing sense of
possibility when moments come, perhaps after weeks,

months or years of hopelessness, and it looks as though life may seem liveable again.

Good Friday Today

Here so much could be said. There are so many experiences and so many sorrows and joys to share. This is, perhaps, one reason why Good Friday is such a remarkable day. By this I do not mean the actual day when Jesus died, but our own memorial of that day, our own Good Fridays each year. There is something about Good Friday and its church services that is remarkable, and one reason for this lies in that common experience of grief. There is a sense in which many people really do feel able to enter into the Good Friday Passion of Christ because it is, in some ways, close to their own passion. Across the country and across the world small and large groups of people gather together, perhaps for an entire three-hour service, dwelling upon the themes of the Passion and death of Christ, or for some shorter period. Individuals may come and go as they are able yet they do not break the unity of the total service. This is, practically, quite unlike all other British church services that expect to begin and end with everyone present. And there is a reason for this. The Good Friday service has about it a depth of personal feeling, a sense of the sincerity of those who came and of those who go. It is deeply personal and yet shared, shared and yet personal. And everyone knows it.

This is a service that probably comes to mean more and more to people as they grow older, for it is with life's events and circumstances that the depth of experience increases. This is, I think, one reason why relatively young members of churches and communities could be encouraged to come to Good Friday services if they have not been familiar with them before. At a time when many churches and even crematoria hold an annual memorial day it is worth pondering the part Good Friday meditations can play in the life of bereaved people. Without being a memorial day for all it is a kind of memorial day, precisely because the death of Christ catches up into itself the pain and death of humankind. The mood of most Good Friday services is, very often, quite different from the great majority of other church events and might even seem slightly odd to recent church members, especially if their usual congregational life is marked by a joyous outpouring of praise. Still, life can only gain from the additional depth brought by each Good Friday's solemn togetherness and its consideration of betrayal and death, two profound aspects of the spirituality of Good Friday.

Betraying and Betrayed

In this chapter it is becoming obvious that the Passion of Christ and his companions reaches into and echoes our own passion, yours and mine. This is why there is a degree of sympathy between us and them. Many of us have not only been betrayed but have, ourselves, betrayed those we love, at least in some way and to some degree. The accounts in the New Testament are not strange stories, foreign experiences. We know about them; they are part of us, and come with us on Maundy Thursday and on Good Friday. As we hear the stories of the many individuals whose paths crossed the journey of Jesus we know they, too, are not strangers to us. We, like them, are betraying and betrayed.

Some of these experiences are major and some are minor, yet they are often, if not always, a partner of love. This is why betrayal is so wounding. It is those who have loved or cared for others, have given themselves in close relationships, that become betrayers and betrayed. Betrayal involves the denial of some degree of love. In betrayal selfishness dominates over self-sacrifice. Care for the other is abandoned and care for self rises powerfully to the surface. The evil of self-love strikes against the love of someone else. This is part of the reason why betrayal of another person also involves a partial betrayal of ourselves. For when someone loves someone else they become part of each other and to deny the other is to deny that part of yourself.

And then there is the person who is betrayed. The one who is surprised, who wonders how the loved spouse, partner or friend could do this to them. How could deceit steal about their relationship in this way, fostering lies and falsehood at every turn? There is a helplessness about life when others lie about us and make a world of pain in which we have to live, whether we like it or not. The sadness of men and women and of our human condition is that this can and does happen. Many know what it is to be part of such circumstances and events. Spite and hatred as well as cold-blooded and calculating deceit can play their parts in this very human scene of betrayal. Scorn, too, breeds its own wicked children.

And as with human relationships so with our religious life. Our own sense of commitment to God may well have been betrayed in many and various ways. We betray God's love sometimes through ignorance, sometimes through weakness, and sometimes by our own deliberate fault, as one of the Church's confessions expresses it. In terms of *The Book of Common Prayer* as it reflected upon this state of sin, 'there is no health in us'. Health and betrayal are, in some senses, linked. At least our sense of well-being and welfare often go hand in hand with our moral and religious condition, though here I must be clear in what I want to say. I am not saying that good health is a reward for being good and that illness is a punishment for being wicked. The Christian understanding of divine love and of the grace of God simply does not work like that. Indeed, one of the most untrue forms of Christianity that has become popular over the last twenty years or so is one that does link health with religious devotion as a kind of reward for services rendered. Similarly, the idea that someone is ill because they have sinned is simply not part of the Christian understanding of cause and effect. What I *am* saying is that human beings live in a world in which our sense of well-being, and ultimately even our health, are very much caught up in the way other people treat us and view us and in the way we view and treat them. It is very hard to draw hard and fast lines between our relationships and our emotions.

So it is that, if we betray a trust and break a relationship or if others do that to us, we do not simply carry on as normal. In our heart of hearts we are affected by what happens, not because God is punishing us, but because we are human and moral persons living in relationships, families and societies where we look for and anticipate fairness and justice. In this word, 'justice', we encounter a giant of an idea. Justice brings a sense of truth into the moral world. It brings order into the otherwise chaotic life of human groups. Justice raises us above the personal concerns, biases and prejudices of daily life. Justice turns fairness into philosophy.

When injustice is done to us we long for it to be put right. There are very many examples of cases of injustice, especially when relatives have had someone murdered, and the culprit is not caught, or the police and authorities do not seem to have done everything in their power to ensure that justice is both done and seen to be done. At such times family members who see themselves as having been wronged talk about their feelings in very physical terms. They may say they feel sick. They have a physical reaction to injustice. This is very much part and parcel of our life and of what we are as social beings. And it is as social beings that betrayal comes to strike us hard for it involves injustice at the most personal of levels. But that is sufficient for us to begin to think about betrayal in our own life and experience, sufficient for us to realise how our passion and that of Christ have at least some elements in common. One reason why the death of Jesus catches our imagination and stimulates faith is because it strikes us as unfair. His betrayal was unfair; his trial was unfair; his death was undeserved. We are offended by it. Yet we also have a sense of its inevitability.

Death

Death is the other main aspect of Good Friday that strikes a chord in our own experience. Perhaps as younger people, or before we have encountered death in those we know and love, our approach to the death of Jesus can, still, be very deep. Our sense of sympathy with his suffering and, perhaps, of gratitude in terms of the belief that he died for us can prompt us to a real devotional response. But perhaps it is also true that those whose own lives have involved suffering, whether through serious or chronic illness or through bereavement, enter into a different level of feeling with Christ. No measurements can be placed on these emotions.

Although it might sound rather obvious it remains true that Christian religion takes death with great seriousness as we saw in the previous chapter. Here, once more, there is a link between our situation and that of Christ. Of course there are several crucial ways in which I would not wish to compare his death and ours. The Christian faith is keen to stress that Christ's death was a sacrifice for sin, and our death is no such sacrifice. His stands as a unique event in the history of the world while our death is unique to us. But it is our own death that I want us to consider now. Indeed, it is hard to avoid any such consideration when we apply ourselves to the Passion of Christ. The very fact that many hymns and biblical passages link his death and ours gives us tremendous opportunity to reflect upon our own mortality in a timely fashion. Death is certain, yet it often takes many years and some specific events or experiences before our own mortality comes before us as a real issue. Once more, it must be said that individuals respond in very different ways to this great question of death. Here I simply want to outline some issues that may be relevant to at least some readers (I have considered other aspects of death at much greater length elsewhere; see Davies 1997).

When we were young, as teenagers, and perhaps even in our early twenties, we felt immortal. Life stretched ahead with all its possibilities. For some this involved opportunities and scope to do many things while, for others, it offered fairly fixed or even limited options as far as employment and family life were concerned. This sense of immortality and possibility is, as likely as not, a very healthy feature of the ambition and drive of young people. It reflects that optimism and hopefulness that underlies human success. When circumstances of unemployment or family circumstances prevent young people from spreading their wings it is unfortunate and a possible stifling of talent. With time, with the onset of an illness, or with the death of a family member or friend we can, fairly rapidly, come to view life in a different way, as something that is of limited duration, that sets boundaries around us. This can be a depressing fact but it is one that needs to be faced, especially by those who fear death and prefer not to think about it. The Passion of Christ calls us to think about death, both his and ours, and to see how we can come to live in the knowledge that we, too, are going to die. In saying this I want to give real emphasis to our death. This is important because it is often the case that clergy find it impossible to talk about the suffering, pain and death of Christ without, immediately, adding on the Easter hope of Resurrection. But that lies beyond the scope of this book. Here I want to allow us the privilege, the Christian privilege, of considering our lives as something of limited extent. Our earthly life ends in death. This should not be ignored as we endeavour to live this life to its full for how we live is influenced by how we think of death. The case of Jesus is instructive on that very point since so much of the teaching associated with his journey to Jerusalem is given in the knowledge that death awaits him.

In Praise of Passion

The silence that grows in us as we ponder the death of Christ will not grow forever. Worship springs from it, a response of identification with him through a sense that he has identified with us. There is something in his hopelessness that fosters our hope. Some of the deepest expressions of Christian faith surround the Passion of Jesus, the man from Nazareth who died at Jerusalem. Among the most powerful of these is an identification of ourselves as those who helped bring this calamity upon him. What happens to Jesus is not strange to us. We know how cruel people can be to each other at the individual and at the political level. Abandonment, torture and cruelty have played as large a part in the last 100 years' history of the world as ever they did before. We can see a truth in his Passion that reflects elements of the truth of our own private passions.

Against this background the argument that Christianity is anti-Semitic when it outlaws Judas needs to be revised. It is true that Judas, whose name means 'Jew', has sometimes been set apart as the greatest of wicked men. It is also true that, at times, he has been taken as a symbol of a 'Jew' in a negative sense. But these are far from the common way of Christian thinking, far from that spirituality in which we see ourselves as the betrayers of Christ. A strong element within Christian tradition encourages believers to see themselves at one with Judas, with Peter, with the rich young ruler and with anyone who betrays Christ.

Hymns of the Passion are example enough of the depth of this feeling. Johann Heerman's (1585–1647) hymn pursues this theme. Its first, second and final verses summarize a wealth of Christian feeling:

> Ah, holy Jesu, how hast Thou offended,
> That man to judge Thee hath in hate pretended?
> By foes derided, by Thine own rejected,
>   O most afflicted.
>
> Who was the guilty? Who brought this upon Thee?
> Alas, my treason, Jesu, hath undone Thee:
> 'Twas I, Lord Jesu, I it was denied Thee:
>   I crucified Thee.
>
> Therefore, kind Jesu, since I cannot pay Thee,
> I do adore Thee, and will ever pray Thee,
> Think on Thy pity and Thy love unswerving,
>   Not my deserving.

Christians have often felt that there must have been extreme depths of experience underlying Christ's Passion that lie beyond our grasp and even beyond imagining. 'There is a deeper pang of grief, / An agony unknown, / In which his Love finds no relief – / He bears it all alone', as T. B. Pollock's hymn, 'Weep Not for Him who Onward Bears his Cross to Calvary', puts it. So too in one of the most popular of nineteenth-century revivalist hymns whose evangelical spirituality can easily be overlooked. Elizabeth Clephane's descriptive song of the Good Shepherd begins, 'There were ninety and nine that safely lay in the shelter of the fold', and tells how the good shepherd goes out in search of the one that was lost. The pursuit of the lost sheep is what happens in the Passion of Christ.

> But none of the ransomed ever knew
> How deep were the waters crossed;
> Nor how dark was the night that the Lord passed
> through
> 'Ere he found his sheep that was lost.

Throughout Christian worship there echoes the highest praise for the Passion of Christ. It taxes the imagination and poetic skills of hymnwriters and springs from the depths of personal suffering. It is strange to speak of praise in connection with Passion and yet that is, in practice, what happens. One of the strange consequences of faith comes from what believers have seen in the suffering and death of Christ. While it is easy to see a simple parallel between the death of Christ and the sacrifice of special animal victims for sin in the Old Testament (and the latter does actually provide a foundation for the Eucharist), that is not the only route of devotion. There is another stream of thought that arises from the human insight into the suffering of another. It is a kind of intuition, an understanding of the power of love and of its consequences. It is this that speaks of Christ standing alongside those who suffer today. It is this that is offered as a response to those great philosophical problems of why God allows suffering. It is not an answer that carries logical power, but it is an insight with its own persuasion.

One of the very best examples of this conviction that the Passion of Christ is, actually, powerful to change human hearts and lives is found in the poetry of G. A. Studdert Kennedy, the famous chaplain of the First World War. His lines would not win poetry prizes and do not fill many

volumes, and yet are one of the first and greatest examples
of what later came to be called the theology of the suffering
God, much explored by the German theologian Jürgen
Moltmann, himself a prisoner of war who learned much
from Studdert Kennedy's work. One of these poems
contrasts the image of God as a heavenly king ruling all
from a safe distance with the Passion of Christ. It is almost
a shame to quote only a few lines from what is a master-
piece of spiritual commitment expressed in verse, but let
these suffice (Studdert Kennedy 1927: 42–43).

> God, the God I love and worship, reigns in sorrow on the
>   Tree,
> Broken, bleeding, but unconquered, very God of God
>   To me.

He then asks where God may truly be found and decides
it is not among the showy splendour, 'all that sheen of
angel wings', but in lowly and ordinary things and, most
especially,

> In the life of one an outcast and a vagabond on earth,
> In the common things He valued, and proclaimed
>   Of priceless worth,
> And above all in the horror of the cruel death he died,
> Thou hast bid us seek Thy glory, in a criminal crucified.
> And we find it – for Thy glory is the glory of Love's loss,
> And Thou hast no other splendour but the splendour of
>   The Cross.

Here Studdert Kennedy reflects a longstanding theme that
grew in strength at the time of the Reformation and,
especially in the thinking of Martin Luther. It is often
called the theology of the cross and it is contrasted with

what is called the theology of glory. The theology of the cross sees the divine nature and its wonder most fully disclosed in the humility of crucified life. Pomp and images of kings and palaces dissolve before the eye of faith and, as Studdert Kennedy sees it as he ends this poem entitled 'High and Lifted Up',

> High and lifted up I see Him on the eternal Calvary
> And two pierced hands are stretching east and west o'er land and sea,
> On my knees I fall and worship that great Cross that shines Above,
> For the very God of Heaven is not Power, but Power of Love.

Such thoughts and responses are more strange than many Christians realise. Familiarity with the images of Christ's suffering and death hide their power. This is why it is worth spending time to ponder them again, to see the contradictions shattering the Master, the Rabbi, as the cluster of betrayals and denials brings him to his shout of forsakenness and to his last cry. It was in the Christian communities that grew out of those who regrouped and felt themselves inspired by Christ's life and presence among them that the power of his Passion came to revive their own passions of denial. For it was the ruptured fellowship of betrayers that became the community rooted in grace. This, perhaps, much more than the customary distinction between grace and works, underpinned and motivated the first Christians. The great divide lies between disciples and Christians: between failure and success, between despair and hope.

Into Temptation and Beyond

It was no accident that the disciples asked Jesus to teach them how to pray. It was no accident that the prayer he gave them was what we have come to know as the Lord's Prayer. This is the single best-known prayer in the history of the Christian world, and probably of the world itself. It is no accident, either, that it includes a petition to 'lead us not into temptation'.

The word for 'temptation' can also mean trial or test. That is why some modern translations of the Lord's Prayer speak of not being brought to the time of trial. One wonders whether this key element of such a central prayer had its own deep significance among the earliest Christians, among those who had known all too well what it was to experience such a time of trial that they had even betrayed and abandoned their Master. If there is any truth in that suggestion we could see how the petition not to be brought to the time of trial is no general and broad desire but an expression grounded in the wisdom of spiritual hindsight.

Throughout this book I have brought together biblical accounts of rejection, betrayal, denial and abandonment in what I called the cluster of betrayal. I have suggested that this cluster reflected a significant element in the spirituality of the earliest Christians and that it touches the life of every generation of believers. Throughout this book it would, just as easily, have been possible to place an equal emphasis upon the idea of trust and to argue that, in betraying Christ's journey, they betrayed his trust which certainly is an undercurrent of the whole story. But that might have detracted from the much more neglected themes of betrayal and denial in Christ's Passion and in ours. At least we have gained an opportunity to see the Church as a company of those who know what they did to him and what he does for them.

Points for Discussion and Reflection

Chapter One Betrayal and Support

1. Where in the New Testament is the early Christian movement described as 'The Way' and how does that description relate to our first chapter?

2. How valuable is it, really, to use the Bible as one way of helping to cope with our life today?

3. Do you find the expression 'family resemblance' useful in the way the chapter tries to link different kinds of rejection and betrayal?

Chapter Two Setting Out and Casting Out

1. Being in control of their life is very important for many people. How does faith relate to that desire?

2. The sense of 'amazement' occurs numerous times in the Gospels. Does it tie in at all with the sense of worship in your experience?

3. Does this chapter influence your own thinking about the rich young ruler?

Chapter Three The Passions of Peter and Pilate

1. What does it mean to say that the Bible was written by people of faith for people of faith?

2. Do you think we tend to gain the whole world and lose our own life in one great act or in many small ones?

3. Is it fair to describe Peter's experience in Acts 10 as his conversion?

Chapter Four The Passion of Judas

1. Numerous scholars see Christianity as an anti-Semitic religion and, because Judas' name actually means 'Jew', see the focus on him as the betrayer of Jesus as a key example of this Christian hostility to Jews. Do you agree with that view?

2. Do you think it wise to ask the question, posed in this chapter, as to whether Judas might have been the first Christian?

3. Would it surprise you to see Judas in heaven?

Chapter Five The Supper

1. Do you think the Judas Cup Ceremony might be of use in churches today?

2. Can you think of the life and teachings of Jesus apart from the group of disciples that followed him? And how does that relate to Christian life today?

3. Is betrayal related to humility?

Chapter Six The Garden Betrayal

1. How could Jesus' disciples possibly have fallen asleep at such a crucial moment?

2. Thinking of the art, the pictures, statues and windows in churches you know or may have visited, how important is the Gethsemane experience of Jesus when compared with other aspects of his life, especially the Crucifixion?

3. How important is art in Christian life?

Chapter Seven Paul's Passion

1. Do you think Paul needed to think of himself as one who betrayed Christ, through his antagonism towards the earliest Christians, in order to compare himself with the actual disciples?

2. Does Christianity dwell too much on ideas of suffering?

Chapter Eight The Death of Christ

1. Is there any sense in which the death of Christ leaves us speechless? If there is, how might the Eucharist reflect this? Perhaps this is to ask if sufficient place is given to silence in many very wordy services?

2. What sense can you make of God forsaking Jesus in the Crucifixion?

3. Which hymns best express the meaning of the death of Christ for you?

Chapter Nine Death's Passion

1. Why are so very few sermons ever preached about death? Is this inevitable in our life-focused world or are there other reasons?

2. How would you describe the mood of Good Friday services? Do you think the Church's year is losing something very worthwhile when this day becomes as ordinary as other days?

Chapter Ten In Praise of Passion

1. What sense do you make of the sacrifice of Christ?

2. Looking back over this book do you see its emphasis upon betrayal as too extreme and, perhaps, misguided or as serving more as a corrective to an absence in much of Christian thinking.

Bibliography

Corr, C. A. (1993) 'Coping with Dying: Lessons We Should and Should Not Learn from the Work of Elisabeth Kübler-Ross', *Death Studies,* 17, 1.

Cranfield, C. E. B. (1966) *The Gospel According to St. Mark* (Cambridge: Cambridge University Press).

Davies, D. J. (1997) *Death, Ritual and Belief* (London: Cassell).

Fitzmyer, J. A. (1981) *The Gospel According to Luke I–IX* (New York: Doubleday).

Goulder, Michael (1989) *Luke: A New Paradigm* (Journal of the Study of the New Testament, 20; Sheffield: JSOT Press).

Maccoby, Hyam (1992) *Judas Iscariot and the Myth of Jewish Evil* (New York: The Free Press).

Marshall, I. Howard (1978) *The Gospel of Luke* (Exeter: Paternoster Press).

Otto, Rudolph (1924) *The Idea of the Holy* trans. J. W. Harvey (Oxford: Oxford University Press).

Quast, Kevin (1989) *Peter and the Beloved Disciple* (Journal of the Study of the New Testament, 32; Sheffield: JSOT Press.

Schweizer, Eduard (1971) *The Good News According to St. Mark* trans. D. H. Madvig (London: SPCK).

Thompson, Francis (1928) *The Hound of Heaven* (London: Burns Oates and Washbourne Ltd).

Index

abandonment, 85, 101, 103
Acts of The Apostles, 8, 28, 40, 82, 93
Adam and Eve, 31, 87
amazement-astonishment, 21, 24, 77
anointing, 25, 51
anti-Semitism, 59, 121
Ash Wednesday, 5, 111
atonement, 101
authority, 34

baptism, 13
Barabbas, 43
Beloved Disciple, 1, 13, 15, 68, 100, 107
bereavement, 112
betrayal-cluster, 2, 6, 14, 17, 25, 33, 48,
    49, 59, 60, 77, 83, 88, 92, 97, 102,
    109, 125, 126
betraying the journey, 6, 10, 12
blasphemy, 83
blood, 65, 70, 101
bread, 70

Calvary, 77
Cana, 29
charisma, 34
church communities, 4, 11, 89
Clephane, E., 122
cluster of betrayal see betrayal-cluster
conversion, 71, 91–92
Corr, C.A., 131
Cranfield, C., 22, 131
cross, 68, 124
crucifixion, 65, 77, 99ff.
cup, 67, 70, 73, 78, 84, 86, 99

death, 110, 111ff., 118ff. 130
denial, 39, 40, 83, 89ff.
devil, 67, 52, 69
despair, 53
disciples, 79, 84, 88, 95, 102, 103, 107,
    108

discipleship, 82
disobedience, 32
Durham Cathedral, 74

Easter Day, 104
El Greco, 31
Elijah, 84, 103
Eucharist, 61, 72ff. 77, 101, 123

family resemblance, 2, 83, 127
faith, 2, 8, 9, 66, 88, 98, 110, 118, 123,
    128
fasting, 13
Father, 69, 100, 101, 103
fear, 22, 24
foot-washing, 67, 68
forgiveness, 34
forsaken, 100, 101ff.
friends-ship, 54–55, 63–64, 68, 84, 99
fundamentalism, 46
funerals, 111

Gethsemane, 7, 67, 68, 73, 77ff., 99,
    112, 129
glory, 66, 69, 124
God, 2, 12, 31, 57, 69, 79, 85, 86, 88,
    105, 106
Gospel, 93
Good Friday, 3, 5, 104, 105, 114ff.
Goulder, M., 102, 131
grace, 70, 95, 96, 109, 117, 125

Hebrews, 30, 88
Heerman, J., 122
Holy Spirit, 8, 30, 34, 82, 93, 107
Hospitality, 67
Humility, 66, 67, 125, 128

identity, 62, 92
illness, 70
interpretation, 11

James and John, 17, 23, 84, 105
Jerusalem, 1, 14, 20, 22, 24, 27, 62
John's Gospel, 8, 13, 51, 52 , 64, 65, 67, 78, 82, 84, 87, 100, 106
Joseph of Arimathea, 108
Judaism, 30
Judas, 12, 26, 49ff., 66, 67, 69, 78, 84, 102, 105, 107, 121, 128
Judas Cup Ceremony, 74
judgement, 70
justice   80, 117

Kennedy, G.A. Studdert, 123
Kingdom of God, 19, 33, 42, 45, 55, 63, 72, 79–83, 98, 103, 109
kiss, 54, 56, 67, 84, 87, 102

Last Supper, 6, 60ff., 101, 107
Lord's Prayer, 126
Lazarus, 27
Lent, 13
loneliness, 108
love, 68, 69, 80, 115, 123
Luther, Martin, 124

Maccoby, Hyam, 59, 131
Mahatma Gandhi, 47
Mary, mother of Jesus, 1, 13–15, 68, 82, 100, 108
Mary, Lazarus' sister, 26
Marshall, H., 15, 28, 131
Maundy Thursday, 3, 73, 115
media, 104
Messiah – Christ, 14, 18, 25, 34, 38, 51, 54, 97
miracles, 33, 37, 99
mocking, 97
Moltmann, Jürgen, 124
mortality, 119
Moses, 84

Nicodemus, 51, 108
numinous, 22

Otto, R., 22, 77, 131

Palm Sunday, 3, 28, 111
Passion of Christ, 10
Passion Sunday, 3
Passover, 29, 50, 51, 60, 61, 65, 73, 84, 100
Passover Lamb, 100

Paul, 2, 12, 39, 70, 88ff., 129
persecution, 92
Peter, 12, 17, 33ff., 68, 84, 105, 107, 122, 128
Pilate, 12, 42ff., 105
Pollock, T.B., 122
postmodernity, 46

Quast, Kevin, 108, 131

rabbi, 79, 86–87
rejection, 20
repentance, 33, 52
resurrection, 21, 29, 39, 41, 53, 90, 91, 104, 120
rich young ruler, 19, 44, 54, 63, 102, 105, 122,127
risk, 104

sacrifice, 53, 81, 100, 119, 123, 130
salvation, 41
Saul-Paul, 91, 92
Schweizer, E., 21, 30, 131
self-sacrifice, 80, 116
shame, 83
silence, 105, 129
Simeon, 14
Simon of Cyrene, 98
Simon-Peter, 35, 39, 85
sin, 53, 71
sleep, 84–85, 102, 129
Son of Man, 39, 75
Stephen, 40, 91
suicide, 55, 113
Synoptic Gospels, 8, 50, 64, 65, 68, 100, 106

Temple, 29, 30, 52, 91, 99
temptation, 85
testimony, 93
theology, 12, 66
Thompson, Francis, 57, 131
transfiguration, 18, 84
trust, 126
truth, 45

vision, 41

Wallinger, Mark, 47
well-being, 116
weeping, 42
worship, 105

Biblical References

Psalms
22:1–11 . . . . . 75, 102
22:31 102
41:9 . . . . 55, 67
55:12–13 55

Matthew
10:33 83
16:18 35
16:46–50 83
19:16–22 54
20:2 26
20:25–28 66
23:37–39 27
26:14 51
26:25 . . . . 50, 64
26:38 84
26:49,50 . . . . 54, 87
27:3–10 . . . . . 50, 52
27:18 44
27:19 53
27:23 53
27:25 44
27:29 53
27:45 100
27:54 53

Mark
1:15 33
1:16 83
1:17 35
1:27 22
2:1–12 34
3:9 83
3:13–19 83
3:31–35 109
4:10–12 33
4:12–16 63
6:7–13 83
6:52 83
8:17 83
8:29 . . . . 17, 37
8:33 . . . . 18, 38
8:36 83
8:38 83
9:2–8 85
9:7 19
9:30–33 19
9:31–32 39
10:15 19
10:22 19
10:23–33 20

10:32 21
10:38 23
10:45 24
10:52 24
11:18 24
11:17 30
14:8 25
14:18 50
14:31 36
14:38 85
14:45 87
14:58 29
14:66–72 39
14:72 37
15:1–15 43
15:19 98
15:26 99
15:34 100
16:9–19 30
19:42–45 66

Luke
2.21–40 15
2:35 14
13:34–35 27
18:18 21
19:41 28
22:22–24 66
22:23 64
22:47 56
22:48 87
24:46 100

John
1:5 50
1:29 65
2:13–22 29
2:20 29
3:19 50
6:35 65
6:44 66
6:51 65
6:66 66
8:12 51
12:6 51
12:1–11 27
13:1 65
13:2 65
13:4–12 66
13:10 67
13:12 . . . . 52, 67
13:21 64

13:23 107
13:27, 30 . . . . 50, 69
13:31 69
13:34 69
14:18 . . . . 95, 107
16:29 82
16:32 . . . . 69, 107
17:21 52
17:22 69
18:1–12 . . . . . 67, 78, 84
18:15 107
18:38 44
19:5 46
19:12 44
19:26–30 . . . . .68, 100
21:19, 22 40

Acts
3:13–14 91
3:17 40
7:52 91
7:53 40
8:1 91
9:4–7 94
9:5 91
9:16 94
10:9–16 41
20:16 93
20:21 93
20:22 93
20:29 93
21:6–10 94
26:12–15 . . . . .91, 92, 94

Romans
1:16 93

1 Corinthians
11:20–21 71
11:23–26 70–71
12:26 94
15:9 91

2 Corinthians
11:23–30 94
12:7–8 94

2 Timothy
2:11–13 90

1 John
2:23 90